IMAGES
of America

SORCERY
IN SALEM

CONTEMPORARY WITCHES AT GALLOWS HILL. The mythological significance of thrice-crossed paths and an ancient tree, the outstretched main limb of which retains a well-worn rope, were chosen by Shawn Poirier to perform an incantation with Lauren M. Doucette. Displayed on the portable altar are an incense container, deer antlers, candles, and various charms that enable him to perform his magic or cast a spell. A third generation witch and the High Priest of the Salem Tradition, Shawn Poirier is a psychic with impressive clairvoyant powers.

IMAGES
of America.

SORCERY
IN SALEM

John Hardy Wright

ARCADIA
PUBLISHING

Published by Arcadia Publishing
Charleston, South Carolina

Library of Congress Catalog Card Number: 99069553

For all general information contact Arcadia Publishing at:
Telephone 843-853-2070
Fax 843-853-0044
E-mail sales@arcadiapublishing.com
For customer service and orders:
Toll-Free 1-888-313-2665

Visit us on the Internet at www.arcadiapublishing.com

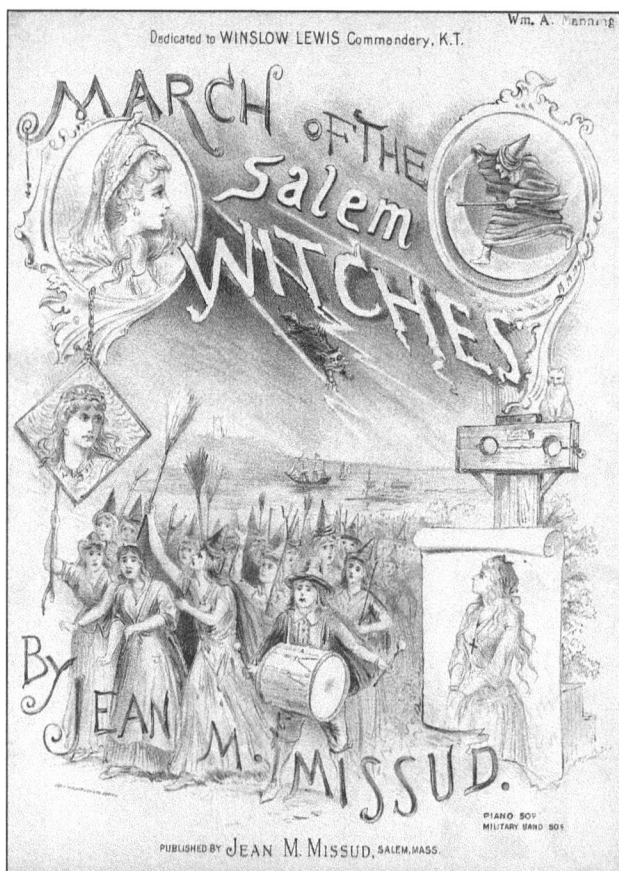

SHEET MUSIC COVER (C. 1908). According to this musical fantasy, a large group of witches has just landed ashore and is marching to some undisclosed location in the city. All the witches in Essex County were seen when their accusers glanced out of the Salem Village Meeting House windows during Martha Cory's examination on March 21, 1692; they were undoubtedly arriving for an unblessed sacrament. One of the bewitched girls asked Goody Cory, "Don't you hear the drum beat?" Jean M. Missud was conductor of the Salem Cadet Band, and Winslow Lewis was commander of the Knights of Templar masonic lodge. (Courtesy Henry R. Theriault.)

CONTENTS

ACKNOWLEDGMENTS

When writing about a subject so far removed in time and one so filled with various accounts by eyewitnesses and secondary sources, an author must acknowledge historians of the past who have endeavored to put the Salem witchcraft episode into perspective. Several insightful books and articles written by mid- to late-20th-century authors are included in the bibliography, and were especially helpful in compiling *Sorcery in Salem*.

This pictorial history could not have been written without the images and objects generously loaned by two local collectors, Stephen J. Schier and Henry R. Theriault, to whom I am ever grateful. Other individuals who helped in one way or another include Jim and Helen Baldwin, Laurie Cabot, Edward Windsor Carberg, Mary A. Cheever, Thomas L. Creamer, David Dunham Sr., Robert D. Farley, Henry Ferrini, Paula Gauthier, Peter George, Joan P. Gormalley, Andrew W. Jackson Jr., Deborah Lathrop, Daniel McDougall, John McDougall, James McIntosh, Bryan McMullin, Peter M. McSwiggin, Victor R. Pisano, Shawn Poirier, Charles A. Potter, Marla Bryerlynne Segal, Robert and Carol Swift, Kathleen Ward, Linda Weinbaum, and Richard D. Wright.

Helpful institutions and the individuals who work for them include the following: Alison C. D'Amario, Director of Education, Salem Witch Museum; Patrick J. Cloherty, Director, and the Reference Room staff, Salem Public Library; Barbara Fanning, Director, Salem Wax Museum of Witches & Seafarers; Prof. David Allen George, Salem State College; Ellen DiGeronimo, Executive Director, and Eileen Konopnicki, Executive Assistant, Salem Chamber of Commerce; K. David Goss, Executive Director, Beverly Historical Society; Dean T. Lahikainen, Curator, and Paula B. Richter, Assistant Curator, American Decorative Arts, Robert E. Saarnio, Curator of Early American Architecture, and Kathy Flynn, Photography Department, Peabody Essex Museum; Thomas H. Neel, Executive Director, and Cari P. Palmer, Director of Marketing and Development, the House of the Seven Gables; Rev. Peter W. Stine, First Baptist Church, Danvers; and Jane E. Ward, Reference Librarian, Phillips Library of the Peabody Essex Museum. Special thanks to Katherine W. Richardson, author of *The Salem Witchcraft Trials* (1983), who edited the completed manuscript.

Photograph credits go to Hartley Ferguson (p. 98), Bill Lane (pp. 113, 115, 116 top, 117,120, 121 top, 122 top, and 123), Bruce Lane (p. 39), Jean Renard (p. 91), and David Spink (p. 94 top).

And lastly, kudos to Patricia Seagreaves, a 10th-grade teacher in Sewell, New Jersey, whose joyful enthusiasm about local history while on sabbatical in Salem has been truly refreshing and illuminating.

This book is dedicated to the memory of Dorothy M. Potter, Librarian at the former Essex Institute, who devoted many of her spare moments in the Institute's archives to document the exact location on Gallows Hill where the hangings occurred.

INTRODUCTION

Occasioned by dreadful witchcraft broke out here a few weeks past,
and one member of this Church, and another of Salem Town,
upon public examination by civil authority suspected for she-witches,
and upon it committed.

When Rev. Samuel Parris added that one awkward sentence to the preface of his sermon book for March 27, 1692, he had no idea of the impact the **dreadful witchcraft** would have on his parishioners **here** (the First Church in Salem Village, now known as Danvers Highlands). Parris, the fourth minister, would be a central player in an ongoing historic drama that would affect the lives of 157 imprisoned victims, 20 of whom were executed, during the summer and fall of that year.

The warm hearth of the Parris parsonage during the bitterly cold winter of 1691–92 (a leap year) became, when the strict Calvinist parents were away, an incubator of the occult for a group of inquisitive adolescent girls and nine-year-old Betty Parris. She, her eleven-year-old orphaned cousin, Abigail Williams, and the other girls were entertained with voodoo tales by an alleged sorceress named Tituba. An Amerindian slave, Tituba and her husband, John Indian (their race, not their surname), were brought to America by Parris when he left his inherited, yet failing, plantation on Barbados. The initial hysterical outbursts of the "afflicted children" (as they and later women were called), **a few weeks past**, accompanied by strange contortions, shrieks, and visions of "specters" who tortured them, along with similar "fitts" of others also physically and emotionally harassed, perplexed the villagers, who soon believed the children were bewitched.

Elderly Rebecca Nurse, the one member of this Church, and Martha Cory, another of Salem Town (a bustling seaport about 5 miles from agrarian Salem Village), were both scrutinized upon public examination for unnatural bodily excrescences, referred to as "witches teats," and watched as they interacted with the antic actions of their accusers. The first such examinations by civil authority took place at Lieutenant Nathaniel Ingersoll's ordinary, or tavern, in the heart of Salem Village where Centre and Hobart Streets intersect. Presiding were two magistrates, or justices of the peace, from the town, John Hathorne and Jonathan Corwin. The latter owned the dwelling now referred to as the "Witch House," where many historians have traditionally believed that preliminary examinations occurred in a second-floor chamber.

Economic, social, and political factors, i.e. crop failures, bitter boundary disputes, and long-standing family rivalries (especially between the prolific Putnam and Porter families), combined with redirected rage and dissatisfaction with the Reverend Mr. Parris, fueled the escalating witch hunts. Neighbors in a remote area who should have been compatible with each other were vehemently suspected for she-witches.

7

The malignant maelstrom subsided in late October of 1692 only after the wife of Royal Governor Sir William Phips was accused of witchcraft; he then quickly dissolved the Court of Oyer and Terminer ("to hear and determine"). Some participants in the turbulent trials and swift executions—who may have felt remorse for their involvement—soon penned their thoughts on paper. Most notable was Rev. Cotton Mather, author of *The Wonders of the Invisible World: Being an Account of the Tryals of Several Witches, Lately Executed in New-England*, which was published in London the following year. Well over 300 years after the Salem witchcraft trials and executions—a truly dark side of Colonial American history from which many lessons can be learned—the subject continues to fascinate historians and ordinary people.

Equally fascinating to those who visit the present-day city of Salem, especially in October, are numerous black-clad individuals who practice a different form of witchcraft, a religion called "Wicca." They blend in perfectly with merrymakers who enjoy the almost month-long holiday known as "Haunted Happenings," when museums and fright sights attract everyone, and when on All Hallow's Eve almost 100,000 people parade along festively adorned downtown streets.

Author's Notes: With a few exceptions, 17th-century quotations remain in their original form. Past and present illustrations of "witches flying on broomsticks" in this book were chosen for their historic and decorative appeal, and are not meant to demean persons who practice the religion of witchcraft today. Unattributed artwork in a caption heading is by the author, and an omitted courtesy line indicates that the piece, or postcard, is in the same collection. Unless otherwise indicated, all dates without a year refer to 1692.

WITCHES RECEIVING IMAGES FROM THE DEVIL, FOR USE IN THEIR CHARMS (WOODCUT IN CHAP-BOOKS OF THE EIGHTEENTH CENTURY). The devil that William Barker Sr. of Andover happened upon in the woods in 1689 "had a cloven foot," but was probably not as frightening as this malevolent being who is distributing "poppets" to a coven of witches (called "Evil Angels" by the elderly Reverend John Higginson of the First Church in Salem Town). Winged imps fly over the devil's human emissaries, who made a compact to give him their bodies and souls. The cloven-hoofed, horned beast figure originated with the mythological Greek god Pan, a counterpart to the Roman god Faunus.

One

MALEFICS, MAGISTRATES, AND MINISTERS

EXAMINATION OF A WITCH (1853 OIL PAINTING ON CANVAS BY TOMPKINS H. MATTESON, 1813–1884). In this imaginative mid-19th-century painting with a "Dutch" milieu, the Albany, New York-area artist has included representatives of the four groups of players who interacted with each other in the Salem witchcraft episode of 1692. The accused (those innocent Essex County residents thought to be witches) are stared or pointed at by the swooning young women (the "afflicted children") and others, while the judges have a closer look and make notations. A clergyman or two is included in the cast of characters as one young woman is being examined for a bodily lump, or excrescence. If the "witchmark" bled, and the person cried when pricked, it was considered normal. Such an examination was sanctioned by the clergy, and Cotton Mather believed that a surgeon could determine if a witchmark was magical. (Courtesy Peabody Essex Museum.)

THE MASSACHUSETTS BAY CHARTER, 1629.
Stylized flowers, a lion rampant, the crown
and rose, a unicorn rampant, a fleur-de-lis, and
decorative calligraphy accompany a whimsical
bust-length portrait of King Charles I (reigned
1625–1649) on this important early document.
Massachusetts was established as a Puritan colony
of England, and was self-ruled until 1684, when
this charter was revoked. Up until mid-May of
1692 there was no authority to try capital cases in
the colony or those arrested for practicing felonious
witchcraft. (Collection of Commonwealth of
Massachusetts Art Commission.)

AN ANCIENT WOMAN (19TH-CENTURY ETCHING BY
AN UNIDENTIFIED ARTIST). Goody Mary Glover, an
Irish washerwoman, was held responsible for the
bewitchment of the Goodwin children of Boston
in 1688, for which she was duly executed. Erudite
Cotton Mather owned a book "that proves . . .
That there are Witches . . .," and a contemporary
Boston cloth merchant-historian, Robert Calef,
wrote in 1697 that Goody Glover was "a despised,
crazy, ill-conditioned old Woman . . . [whose]
Answers were Nonsense, and [whose] behavior
[was] like that of one distracted."

REV. COTTON MATHER (1663–1728, OIL PORTRAIT ON CANVAS BY PETER PELHAM, 1684–1751). Youthful stammerer and former medical student Cotton Mather, son of minister Increase Mather, is associated with the witchcraft trials more as an historian than as an observer. In one of his narratives, the young divine wrote that "An army of Devils is horribly broke in upon Salem . . . and the Houses of the good People there are filled with doleful shrieks of their Children and Servants, Tormented by Invisible Hands, with Torture altogether Preternatural." (Courtesy American Antiquarian Society.)

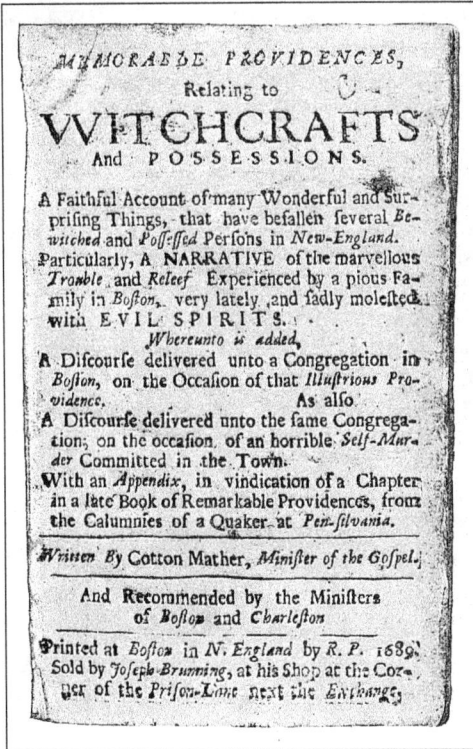

MEMORABLE PROVIDENCES, RELATING TO WITCHCRAFTS AND POSSESSIONS (1689 TITLE PAGE OF NARRATIVE BY COTTON MATHER, PUBLISHED IN BOSTON). The hunting for, and the burning of, untold thousands of witches in Europe during the 16th and 17th centuries was unparalleled. England's last execution by hanging for witchcraft happened in 1682, seven years before the Reverend Mr. Mather wrote this history about the bewitchment of the Goodwin children, and 10 years before the unique hysteria that afflicted Salem. (Courtesy Salem Public Library.)

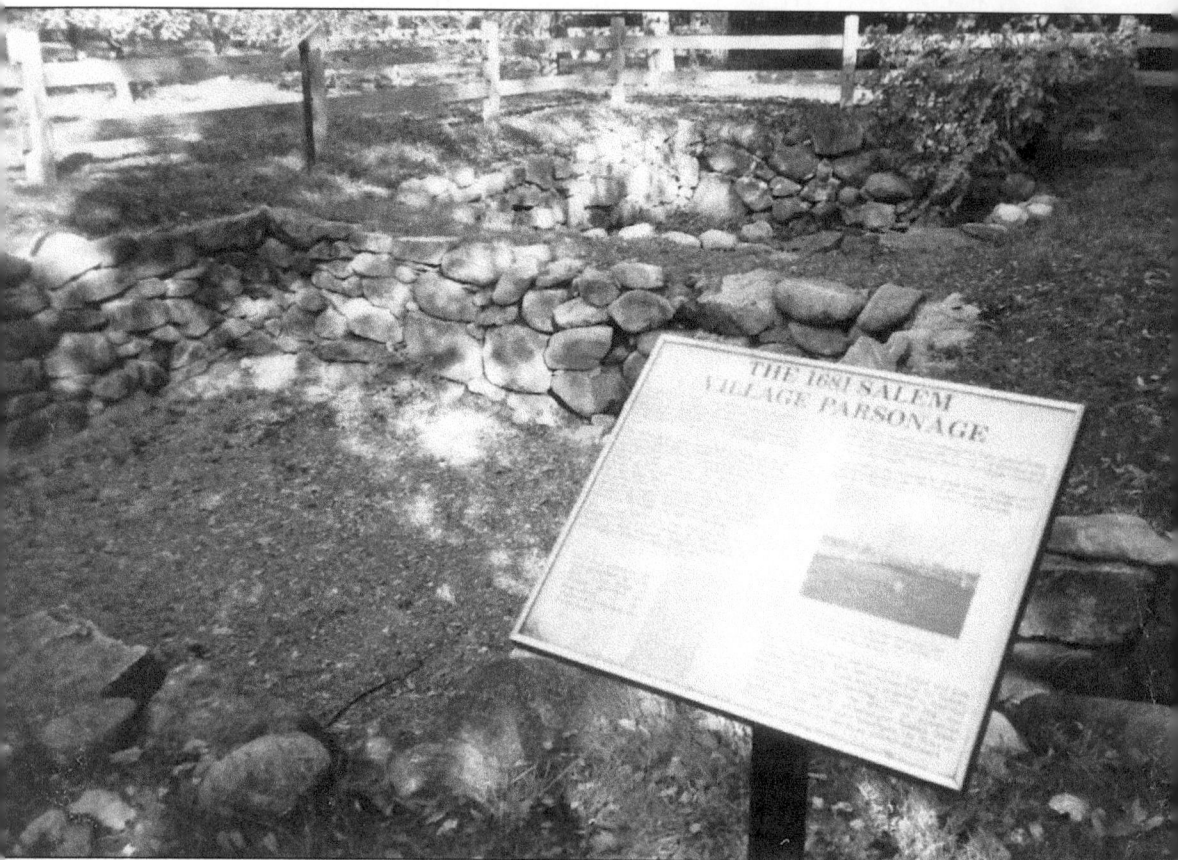

THE SAMUEL PARRIS ARCHAEOLOGICAL SITE, BEHIND 67 CENTRE STREET, DANVERS HIGHLANDS. Excavation of the wood-framed remains of the residence of Rev. Samuel Parris and his family was begun in late July of 1970 with professional archaeologists and interested townspeople. Built in 1681, the southern-exposed dwelling measured 42 by 20 feet, and had a lean-to at the rear. Many shards of objects and bits and pieces of everyday life during the Colonial period came to light, and the stone foundation walls were reassembled. Now a town park, the site has informative signage with appropriate illustrations to document the structure and its history until it was razed in 1784. The Reverend Mr. Parris wrote that "when these Calamities first began, [in the winter of 1692], which was in my own Family, the Affliction was several weeks before such hellish Operations as Witchcraft were suspected." The Parris archaeological site is in the Salem Village Historic District, about midway between the two blue and yellow metal identification signs at the junction of Holten and Collins Streets (where the 1670 Judge Samuel Holten House is located) and near the junction of Route I95 on Centre Street.

TITUBA TEACHING THE FIRST ACT OF WITCHCRAFT (C. 1892 WASH DRAWING BY AN UNIDENTIFIED ARTIST IN *WITCHCRAFT ILLUSTRATED*). Many historians have written that the rod Tituba is using to inscribe a witch's circle on the sanded floor should have been used on the children instead. In addition to Betty and Abigail, the other girls—Ann Putnam Jr. (12), Mary Walcott (16), Elizabeth Hubbard (17), Susannah Sheldon (18), Elizabeth Booth (18), Mercy Lewis (19), and Mary Warren (20)—were "Getting into Holes, and creeping under Chairs and Stools . . . [exhibiting] sundry odd Postures and Antick Gestures [while], uttering foolish, ridiculous Speeches, which neither they themselves nor any others could make sense of . . ." Thus wrote early historian Robert Calef in *More Wonders of the Invisible World* (London, 1700). Dr. William Griggs, the first physician in Salem Village, after examining the girls in February, exclaimed that "The evil hand is upon them."

REV. SAMUEL PARRIS (1653–1720, MINIATURE ON IVORY BY AN UNIDENTIFIED ARTIST). A Harvard College drop-out who was ordained only three years before the witchcraft hysteria began, Parson Parris served as the fourth Salem Village minister for eight abysmal years (beginning in 1689), during which time he made many enemies. One of his sermons (John 6:70) fanned the flames of witchcraft when he stated that "Jesus answered them [the disciples], Have not I chosen you twelve, and one of you is a devil?" Not an exceptional minister nor an effective sermonizer, Parris is regarded by most historians as an instigator, not an ameliorator. (Courtesy Massachusetts Historical Society.)

DETAIL OF AN UNTITLED SILHOUETTE (1808, LONDON). This image is used to represent the baking of a "witch cake" around February 25 by John Indian upon the suggestion of Mary Sibley, aunt of Mary Walcott. An admixture of the girls' urine and rye meal, the cake was fed to a dog "as a means to Discover witchcraft." If the dog acted erratically, it would prove that they were bewitched. Other experiments included dropping an egg white into a glass of water (forerunner of a crystal ball) and the sieve and shears (a type of divining, somewhat akin to a ouija board).

FIRST MEETINGHOUSE (1874 WOODCUT IN *HISTORY OF THE FIRST PARISH, DANVERS, MASS*). Salem Village became a separate parish of Salem Town in 1672, and the following year this simple wood-framed meetinghouse was raised. Both religious and civil gatherings were held in the structure, which was located at the corner of Hobart and Forest Streets, until it was dismantled and razed in 1702. Salem Town magistrates John Hathorne and Jonathan Corwin conducted the first prosecuting examinations of witchcraft suspects there on March 1, 1692. Sarah Good and Sarah Osburn were interrogated separately, followed by Tituba, whose imaginative revelations elicited further investigations.

A REPRODUCTION OF THE 1672 MEETINGHOUSE, THE REBECCA NURSE HOMESTEAD, 149 PINE STREET, DANVERS HIGHLANDS. Professionals and volunteers erected this adaptation of the first religious structure in Salem Village as a "prop" for the 1985 film *Three Sovereigns for Sarah*. On Sunday afternoon, August, 16, 1992, a commemorative program was held inside the building to mark the 300th anniversary of the deaths of George Jacobs Sr., Rev. George Burroughs, and three other persons executed for supposedly practicing witchcraft. The building has since been used to interpret the historic site with a sound and light program.

15

THE FIRST CHURCH OF CHRIST, 41 CENTRE STREET, DANVERS HIGHLANDS (C. 1892 PHOTOGRAPH BY FRANK COUSINS). The sixth church of this religious society—a Shingle-style edifice with a tall bell tower, built in 1890 after plans by Boston architect Arthur H. Vinal—was unfortunately destroyed by fire in 1978. The present First Church of Christ, Congregational, was built two years later according to plans drawn by local architect Robert D. Farley. Puritans considered the "church" to be those elect individuals who could receive communion, not the building itself. While in prison, Andover witch William Barker Sr. wrote a confession to the magistrates that confirmed what ministers in Salem and Boston believed, namely that the devil had as his "design . . . to Destroy Salem Village, and to begin at the Ministers House, and to destroy the Church of God, and to set up Satans Kingdom, and then all will be well." (Courtesy Stephen J. Schier.)

THE SITE OF THE FIRST CHURCH, CORNER OF HOBART AND FOREST STREETS, DANVERS HIGHLANDS. There were about 90 households in this area in the early 1690s containing approximately 215 persons over the age of 21. The dwellings were randomly situated, with most facades facing the winter sun. Narrow sliding sash fenestration and other early architectural features would date the present structure to the "First Period," even if research did not uncover the first owner's name, John Darling, and its 1680s date of construction. It was moved to this site in the 19th century.

THE PRINCE-OSBURN HOUSE, 273 MAPLE STREET, DANVERS (C. 1892 PHOTOGRAPH BY FRANK COUSINS). This c. 1680 dwelling was home to an ailing, bed-ridden scold, Sarah Prince Osburn, who had a checkered past and who, as a widow, lived openly with a hired man until they were wed. Built by her first husband, Robert Prince, on Spring Street, the house was moved and renovated c. 1914. Convicted of practicing witchcraft, Sarah Osburn died in a Boston prison on May 10—the first victim of the hysteria—one month before Bridget Bishop was executed. (Courtesy Schier Collection.)

THE THOMAS AND ANN PUTNAM HOUSE (C. 1892 PHOTOGRAPH BY FRANK COUSINS). Built at 177 Dayton Street, this house was later removed to the grounds of the Danvers State Hospital. A later-generation Putnam and his wife pose with the family dog near the side entrance wherein (a few years after 1692) lived Sgt. Thomas Putnam Jr. (a supporter of the Reverend Mr. Parris), Thomas' emotionally disturbed and sickly wife, Ann Carr Putnam (referred to as "Sr." in documents), and their daughter Ann ("Jr."). When Martha Cory visited the Putnams in their previous home to see the girl who had accused her of practicing witchcraft, Ann became fitful and screamed that Goody Cory's specter was roasting a man on a spit. (Courtesy Schier Collection.)

ARRESTING A WITCH (1883 ILLUSTRATION IN *HARPER'S NEW MONTHLY MAGAZINE* BY HOWARD PYLE, 1853–1911). In 1831, Boston historian James Thacher wrote the following description of unfortunate elderly women who were accused of witchcraft: "A witch, in her personal character, was commonly an uncouth old woman, or hag. Her countenance was repulsive, her air and gait disgusting, and her general aspect and movements at variance with proper demeanor." Bad Goody Good became a beggar after she suffered financial problems; she possessed a sharp tongue, smoked a pipe, and was "so turbulent a spirit, spiteful, and so maliciously bent."

ACCUSATION OF A BEDEVILED GIRL (1892 ILLUSTRATION IN *HARPER'S NEW MONTHLY MAGAZINE* BY HOWARD PYLE). A domino effect of diabolical molestations caused the "afflicted children" to wail and scream in both meetinghouse and later courtroom situations. They were visibly shaken, incurred temporary loss of hearing, their speech was impaired as was their sight, and they suffered loss of memory. Some present-day historians think they were plagued with ergotism, a mold in bread that may have led to hallucinations, but that is highly doubtful as countless others in the community would also have eaten rye bread with their meals. A "globus hystericus" (contraction of the throat) appears to have silenced the maiden in the foreground, and terrifying visions affect the other witch-hunters, who were described by George Jacobs Sr. as "bitch witches." One of the young women stated that at the devil's sacrament witches drank their victims' blood twice per day, and that they feasted on red bread and red wine as well.

19

SATAN THE SEDUCER (C. 1831 UNTITLED WOOD ENGRAVING BY AN UNIDENTIFIED ARTIST IN JAMES THACHER'S *AN ESSAY ON DEMONOLOGY, GHOSTS AND APPARITIONS, ALSO, AN ACCOUNT OF THE WITCHCRAFT DELUSION AT SALEM IN 1692*). Satan, God's fallen angel, is depicted here as a visually abhorrent satyr-like figure with scaled horns, demonic eyes, pointed teeth, and strange, animal-like, shaggy elbows. He has many evil-sounding titles including "his Satanic majesty," "the crafty one," "The Father of Lies," "Old Nick," "The Old Boy," and the "Prince of Darkness." Boston divines Samuel Wardwell and Cotton Mather referred to him as "the black man" and branded him and witches "night-birds." Salem Village ministers Deodat Lawson and Samuel Parris called him the "Fountain of Malice" and nicknamed him "the old dragon" and "the roaring lion." Sarah Osburn described the devil as "a thing like an Indian all black," thereby combining threefold the fear of Native Americans, persons of color (Tituba), and witches. (Private Collection.)

20

THE WITCH HOUSE, 310 1/2 ESSEX STREET, SALEM (C. 1885 PEN-AND-INK DRAWING IN *SOUVENIR OF SALEM, MASS.*). Five gables, three of which feature a finial, in shape not dissimilar from a pineapple (the symbol of hospitality), adorn the dimensional façade of this historic home. A projecting two-story enclosed porch with arched batten door has several casement windows for side illumination, with other fenestration likewise symmetrical. The clustered brick chimney and pendants are also hallmarks of Elizabethan structures in both England and New England. Judge Jonathan Corwin, the son of merchant George Corwin and the uncle of Sheriff George Corwin, contracted with bricklayer Daniel Andrew in 1674–75 to remodel the existing dwelling on the site, thought to have been constructed after 1642. Some of the rooms were to feature blue-and-white Dutch tiles, probably surrounding the fireplace openings. (Courtesy Schier Collection.)

A Portion of the Cellar of the Old Witch Jail, formerly Located at 4 Federal Street, Salem (C. 1936 POSTCARD). Many of the accused and condemned witches were imprisoned in this cold, dank jail (built in 1684, it was about 20 feet square by 13 feet high). Others were incarcerated in Ipswich and Boston jails, which soon became overly crowded. Four-year-old Dorcas Good, "dafter" of Sarah, was imprisoned, as were numerous pregnant and elderly women. Although it is thought that there were no bars in the jail, iron shackles prevented the witches from escaping; the families of the witches had to pay for those shackles and food while their loved ones were confined. (Courtesy Theriault Collection.)

Witch Pins (C. 1892 PHOTOGRAPH BY FRANK COUSINS). Several pins were placed in this small, clear glass bottle (probably during the mid- to late 19th century), and they then took on the significance of historic relics. The pins were preserved among the files of the Essex County Superior Court in Salem. Although "the accused were charged with using them to torment their victims"—Mary Warren had cried out against Mary Parker when "a pin run through her hand [caused] blood runeing out of her mouth"—they may actually have fastened together some of the witchcraft documents. (Courtesy Schier Collection.)

THE PHILIP ENGLISH HOUSE, FORMERLY LOCATED AT THE CORNER OF ESSEX AND ENGLISH STREETS (C. 1823 WASH DRAWING BY MISS E.W. DALRYMPLE AND JOHN R. PENNIMAN). One of Salem Town's wealthiest merchants, Philip English, was arrested in Boston in late April where he had been in seclusion after being "called out." Both he and his wife, Mary Hollingsworth English, also accused of witchcraft, escaped to New York. Sheriff Corwin in the name of the Crown of England seized their c. 1690 grand mansion house (razed in 1833) and valuable property, estimated at about £1500.

THE LEWIS HUNT HOUSE, FORMERLY LOCATED AT THE CORNER OF WASHINGTON AND LYNDE STREETS (C. 1860 STEREOPTICON VIEW). Resembling the "Witch House," the c. 1698 Hunt House was a venerable landmark in downtown Salem until it was razed in 1863. Residents could walk out the front door, or peer out of its side windows, adjacent to the first courthouse in the middle of Washington Street. The court chambers on the second floor were first used as such in May of 1679, and were where the witchcraft trials were held; a school was on the first floor. (Courtesy Theriault Collection.)

23

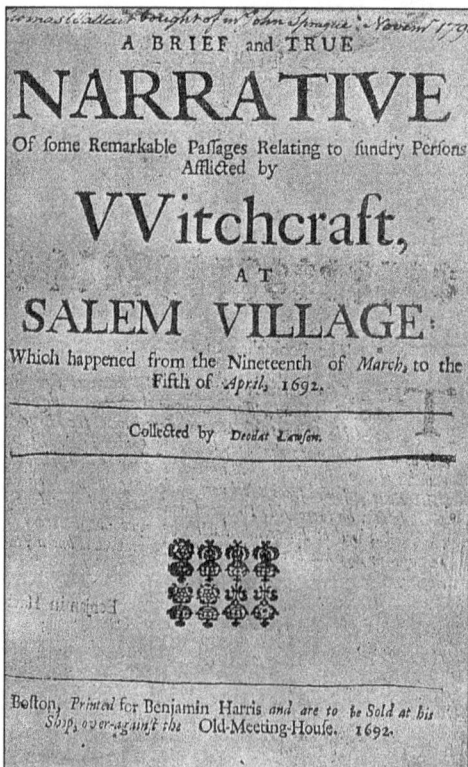

A BRIEF and TRUE

NARRATIVE

Of fome Remarkable Paffages Relating to fundry Perfons
Afflicted by

VVitchcraft,

A T

SALEM VILLAGE

Which happened from the Nineteenth of *March*, to the
Fifth of *April*, 1692.

Collected by *Deodat Lawfon.*

Bofton, *Printed* for Benjamin Harris *and are to be Sold at his
Shop, over-againft the* Old-Meeting-Houfe. 1692.

LAND HO! (MID-18TH-CENTURY ENGRAVING OF A VESSEL TO REPRESENT THE *NONESUCH*). An early American diplomat to England, Rev. Increase Mather accompanied Sir William Phips, the newly appointed royal governor of the Massachusetts Bay Colony, to Boston on May 14, 1692, with the new royal charter. The charter enabled Phips to establish a special court to try the backlog of witchcraft cases. The Court of Oyer and Terminer was set up on May 27, and on June 15, 12 ministers reported their findings regarding spectral evidence to said court.

A BRIEF AND TRUE NARRATIVE (1692 TITLE PAGE OF DEODAT LAWSON'S PAMPHLET, PUBLISHED IN BOSTON). Among other observations, the third minister of the church in Salem Village wrote of the hysterical girls that their "motions in their fitts are preternatural, being much beyond the ordinary force of the same person when they are in their right minds." The Reverend Mr. Lawson is associated with the first spectral image—a yellow bird seen perched on his hat before the reverend minister delivered a sermon on March 20. (Courtesy Salem Public Library.)

"Thou Shalt Not Suffer A Witch To Live"

Exodus xxii, 18

A BIBLICAL INJUNCTION (C. 1886 PEN-AND-INK DRAWING BY FRANK T. MERRILL IN *LYNN AND SURROUNDINGS*). The first person to be executed in Salem Town for practicing witchcraft was Bridget Bishop, a termagant in her fifties who had been called a witch by one of her neighbors as early as 1678. Bridget was thought to have bewitched her first husband, Goodman Oliver, to death. While in her cellar, two workmen discovered "poppets" with hogs' bristles and sharp pins, supposedly used to inflict her victims. (Courtesy Schier Collection.)

GALLOWS HILL, SALEM (C. 1888 ETCHING BY GEORGE M. WHITE, 1849–1915). Historians of the 19th and 20th centuries have tried to determine exactly where on the western side of the hill the visible executions occurred. One plausible location is the rocky area around Pope Street, almost opposite the end of Federal Street. Twelve years after 1692, at an execution elsewhere, Samuel Sewall described the raising of the scaffold and how the women in attendance screamed when it was lowered. It is possible that a scaffold may have been used on Gallows Hill in 1692 instead of a tree.

THE MEMORIAL TO BRIDGET BISHOP, SALEM WITCH TRIALS MEMORIAL, NORTHLIBERTY STREET. During her examination on April 19, Bridget Bishopstated "I am innocent to a witch [and] I know not what a Witch is . . . I have no familiarity with the devil."

The Death Warrant and Execution of Bridget Bishop (c. 1892 photograph by Frank Cousins). On the second of June, the wife of sawyer Edward Bishop was indicted and arraigned for practicing witchcraft on several of the afflicted young women and men. Although she pleaded "not guilty," Bridget Bishop was charged and was sentenced to death for that felony. Sometime between the hours of 8 and 12 on June 10, Bridget Bishop was taken "to the place of Execution and . . . [was] hanged by the neck until she be de[ad]." Shortly thereafter, Judge Nathaniel Saltonstall of Haverhill resigned from the court in dismay, making him the first to decry total reliance on spectral evidence. (Collection Peabody Essex Museum.)

THE REBECCA NURSE HOUSE, 149 PINE STREET, DANVERS HIGHLANDS. Situated picturesquely on a small knoll of land that now encompasses about 27 acres, this First Period red farmhouse is on property initially owned by Townsend Bishop in 1636. Gov. John Endicott purchased the land in 1648, and by 1678—the traditional construction date carved with the initials "TB" inside the sundial over the front door—then-owner James Allen began renting it to tray maker Francis Nurse, who along with his children purchased the property at the end of 20 years. The lean-to, or saltbox, house had been in the Putnam family since 1784, and its restoration was begun in 1908 by the Rebecca Nurse Memorial Association. The Society for the Preservation of New England Antiquities acquired the property in 1926, and in 1981 it was transferred to the Danvers Alarm List Company, Inc.

Rebecca Nurse, as Portrayed by Mrs. Lawrence Waters Jenkins (c. 1926 photograph). The 71-year-old Rebecca, mother of eight, watched neighbors from her bedchamber as officials approached the family home to arrest her for practicing witchcraft. Ironically, her mother, Rebecca Towne, had been accused of the same felony in the past; at her trial Mrs. Nurse stated, "I can say before my Eternal father I am innocent, & God will clear my innocency." Lying was anathema to Calvinist Puritans, and since the devil was known as the "Prince of Lies," a person could be accused of a false confession regarding witchcraft.

The Depositions of Ann Putnam Sr. and Ann Putnam Jr., May 31, 1692 (c. 1892 photograph by Frank Cousins). One of 48 depositions in which the younger Putnam's name appears, these statements relate to the "tormentors" Rebecca Nurse, her sister, Sarah Cloyce, and Martha Cory. The direct, guilt-presuming question, usually asked by Magistrate Hathorne, "Who is it that afflicts you?", prompted the frenzied females to point their fingers at those in the community, such as Goody Nurse, whom they may have envied or despised. Acquitted initially, the matriarch of the Nurse family was then sentenced to death by the jury; Governor Phips later rescinded his order for her pardon. (Collection Peabody Essex Museum.)

THE TRIAL OF GEORGE JACOBS, AUGUST 5, 1692 (1855 OIL PAINTING ON CANVAS BY TOMPKINS H. MATTESON). The Victorian artist's sequel painting depicts the elderly, red-cloaked Jacobs on bended knee with one of his two canes by his side, in the midst of a tumultuous courtroom scene. The judges are trying to question him while his afflicted victims "die away," i.e. faint. In his testimony, teenager John DeRich agreed with the afflicted girls when he stated that "the prisoner Knockt me down with his stafe." Lacking legal experience to handle such indictments, the magistrates listened to the clergy's counsel and their own voices when it came to dealing with spectral evidence; however, they overwhelmingly condemned "those who were accused of spectral evidence" as the jails were being filled to capacity. In 1692, 153 people from the greater Salem area were apprehended. Serving under Deputy Governor William Stoughton of Boston, who was named chief justice, were Bostonians Maj. John Richards, Peter Sargent, Samuel Sewall, and Wait Winthrop; Nathaniel Saltonstall of Haverhill; and beside the aforementioned Jonathan Corwin and John Hathorne, there was Maj. Bartholomew Gedney, also of Salem Town. (Courtesy Peabody Essex Museum.)

THE GEORGE JACOBS SR. HOUSE, FORMERLY LOCATED ON WATER STREET IN DANVERSPORT (C. 1892 PHOTOGRAPH BY FRANK COUSINS). Richard Waters probably built this farmhouse, which was purchased by George Jacobs Sr. around 1658. It remained in the family until around 1920. After Mr. Jacobs was imprisoned, Sheriff Corwin and his associates seized the property and Mrs. Jacobs' wedding ring (temporarily), forcing her to purchase provisions from the sheriff and then accept donations of foodstuffs from neighbors. (Courtesy Schier Collection.)

THE JOHN PROCTOR SR. HOUSE, 348 LOWELL STREET, PEABODY (MID-19TH-CENTURY WOODCUT). During this period, the former residence of the Proctor family presented a rural appearance, one where weary travelers could rest on the tree seats by the side of the road. Events that led to the death of John Proctor Sr. are the subject of Arthur Miller's 1953 play *The Crucible*. The sons of executed Andover resident Martha Carrier, the "Queen of Hell," confessed under duress that their mother was a witch; while in jail they were "tyed . . . Neck and Heels till the Blood was ready to come out of their Noses."

WITCHCRAFT VICTIMS ON THE WAY TO GALLOWS HILL (MAY 14, 1930 ILLUSTRATION IN SUPPLEMENT TO *THE BOSTON HERALD* BY F.C. YOHN). After witnessing the five executions on August 19, Bostonian Thomas Brattle wrote that "With great affection . . . they [the victims] prayed that God would discover what witchcrafts were among us . . . they forgave their accusers . . . and seemed to be very sincere, upright, and sensible of their circumstances on all accounts . . . especially Proctor and Willard, whose whole management of themselves, from the Gaol to the Gallows . . . was very affecting and melting to the hearts of some considerable Spectatours." (Courtesy Theriault Collection.)

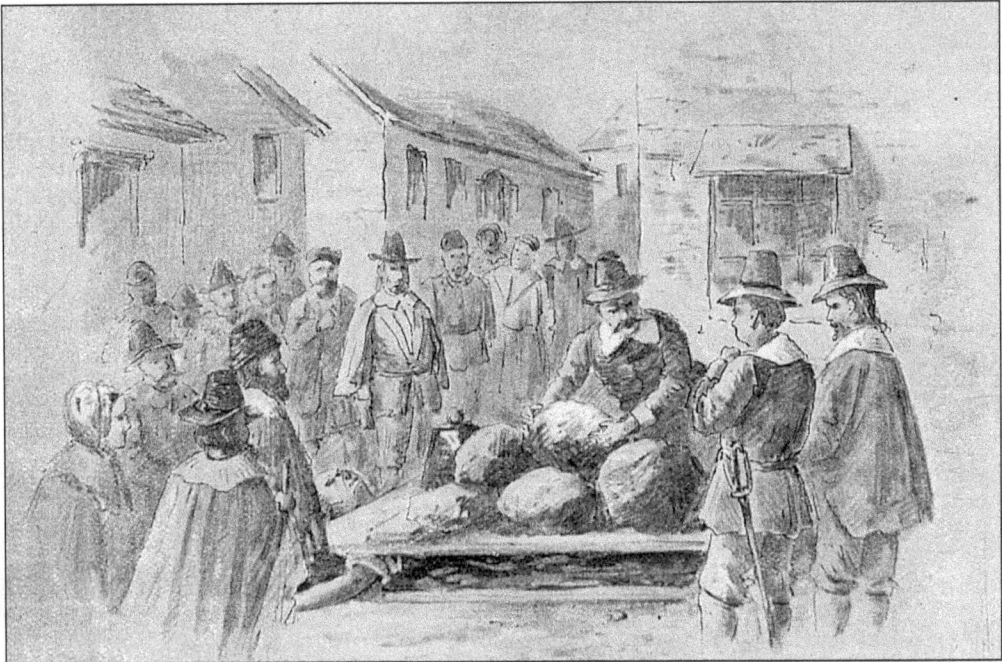

GILES CORY'S PUNISHMENT AND AWFUL DEATH (C. 1892 WASH DRAWING BY AN UNIDENTIFIED ARTIST IN *WITCHCRAFT ILLUSTRATED*). On September 19, three days before the death of his wife, Martha, and other innocents, unpopular octogenarian and "dreadful wizard" Giles Cory was "Prest unto Death, because of his Refusing to Plead for his Life." Remaining mute, Cory suffered "peine forte et dure" (extreme and lengthy pain) as a personal protest to the proceedings of the court. According to legend, the unmerciful Sheriff Corwin pushed the dying man's tongue back into his mouth as he lay under the increasing weight. Giles Cory managed to utter "More weight" before he expired; his crushed body was thrown in a nearby ditch, which during the 19th century became the Howard Street Cemetery.

THE LAST OF THE SALEM WITCHES, WITCH DUNGEON MUSEUM, 16 LYNDE STREET. On September 22, seven witches and one wizard (Samuel Wardwell—he was only arrested three weeks before his death) were executed on Gallows Hill. Most of the eyewitnesses to the unparalleled event were appalled, with the exception of the afflicted young women, who were still being frantically tormented by unseen demons. Before departing the gruesome spectacle, Rev. Nicholas Noyes of Salem Town turned to the bodies dangling from the locust or oak tree(s), and was heard to remark, "What a sad thing it is to see Eight Firebrands of Hell hanging there." About 40 people who confessed to practicing witchcraft were spared. The last victim of the witchcraft hysteria was Lydia Dastin of Reading, who expired in a Boston prison on March 10, 1693.

THE MEMORIAL TO MARY EASTY [SIC], SALEM WITCH TRIALS MEMORIAL, NORTH LIBERTY STREET. The following list documents the victims of the Salem witchcraft episode and the dates they were executed:

June 10: Bridget Bishop, Salem Town

July 19: Sarah Good, Salem Village
Elizabeth How, Topsfield
Susannah Martin, Amesbury
Rebecca Nurse, Salem Village
Sarah Wilds, Topsfield

August 19: Rev. George Burroughs, Wells, Maine
Martha Carrier, Andover
George Jacobs Sr., Salem Farmes
John Proctor Sr., Salem Farmes
John Willard, Salem Village

September 19: Giles Cory, Salem Farmes

September 22: Martha Cory, Salem Farmes
Mary Esty, Topsfield
Alice Parker, Salem Town
Mary Parker, Andover
Ann Pudeator, Salem Town
Wilmot Redd, Marblehead
Margaret Scott, Rowley
Samuel Wardwell, Andover

INCREASE MATHER (1639–1723, OIL ON CANVAS COPY BY CUNNINGHAM AFTER THE PORTRAIT BY JOB VAN DER SPRIETT). Rev. Increase Mather, a former president of Harvard College, diplomat, and pastor of the North Church in Boston, attended a meeting of fellow divines in Cambridge on October 3, shortly after the last executions in Salem Town, where he made a strong point opposing the use of spectral evidence. Mather stated that "It were better that ten suspected Witches should escape, than that one innocent Person should be Condemned." Spectral evidence was soon negated by Governor Phips; the Court of Oyer and Terminer was terminated on October 29, and in May of 1693 he ordered all remaining suspected witches freed from prisons. (Courtesy American Antiquarian Society.)

THE GRAVESTONE OF REV. JOHN HALE (1636–1700), ABBOTT STREET CEMETERY ("ANCIENT BURIAL GOUND"), BEVERLY. Chosen as pastor of the First Church in Beverly in 1665, the Reverend Mr. Hale shepherded his flock for over 30 years, and was regarded as "a pious and faithful minister of ye gospel." Two years after the witchcraft episode he had a house built at 39 Hale Street, where he lived until passing on to his reward.

SAMUEL SEWALL (19TH-CENTURY ENGRAVING COPIED FROM THE MASSACHUSETTS HISTORICAL SOCIETY'S 1728 OIL PORTRAIT BY NATHANIEL EMMONS, 1704–1740). The "Blame and Shame" that Judge Sewall (1652–1730) felt for his part in the witchcraft proceedings was read to parishioners of the Old South Meeting House in Boston by Rev. Samuel Willard. Prayers and fasting occurred on January 14, 1697, a "Day of Humiliation." Twelve jurymen also apologized for any wrong-doings in a printed document as "we would none of us do such things again on such grounds for the whole world . . ."

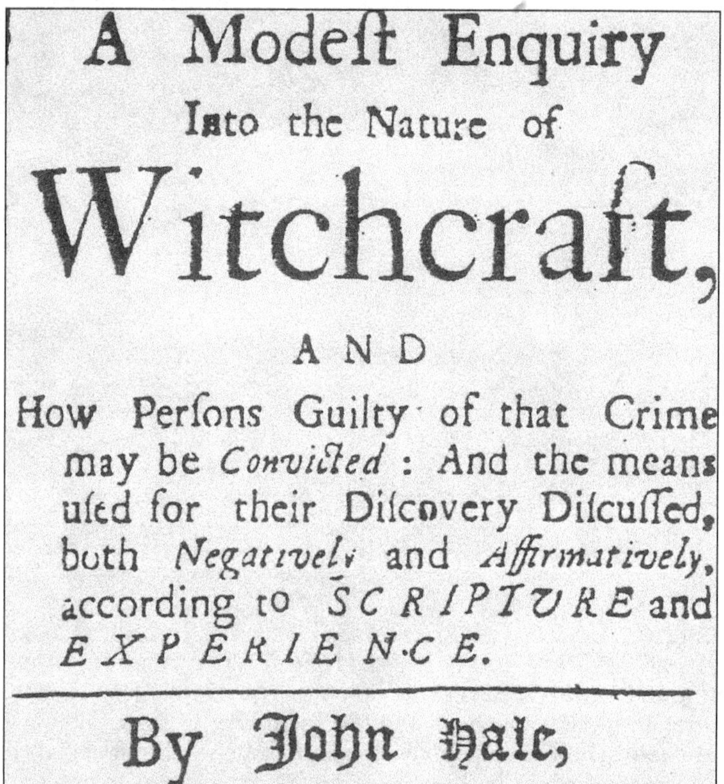

A Modeſt Enquiry
Into the Nature of
Witchcraft,

AND

How Perſons Guilty of that Crime may be *Convicted*: And the means uſed for their Diſcovery Diſcuſſed, both *Negatively* and *Affirmatively*, according to *SCRIPTURE* and *EXPERIENCE*.

By John Hale,

Paſtor of the Church of Chriſt in *Beverley*,
Anno Domini. 1697.

When they ſay unto you, ſeek unto them that have Familiar Spirits and unto Wizzards, that peep, &c. To the Law and to the Teſtimony; if they ſpeak not according to this word, it is becauſe there is no light in them, Iſaiah VIII. 19, 20.
That which I ſee not teach thou me, Job 34. 32.

BOSTON in N. E.
Printed by *B. Green*, and *J. Allen*, for *Benjamin Eliot* under the Town Houſe: 1702

A MODEST ENQUIRY (1697 TITLE PAGE OF A SMALL BOOK WRITTEN BY JOHN HALE, PUBLISHED POSTHUMOUSLY IN 1702). An eyewitness to many of the events in Salem Village and Salem Town, the Reverend Mr. Hale wanted to record the facts for posterity as he remembered them. He didn't doubt that witchcraft was being practiced locally, and later realized (after his wife, Sarah, had been called out before November 5) that he, the magistrates, and others were terribly wrong in their judgment of the victims. Both Hale and Cotton Mather blamed the whole episode on "conjurations" and "vain curiosity" of the "singlewomen." (Courtesy Beverly Historical Society.)

THE CHURCH IN SALEM VILLAGE HISTORIC MARKER, CORNER OF CENTRE AND HOBART STREETS. Rev. Joseph Green, Samuel Parris' youthful replacement, read Ann Putnam Jr.'s "confession" from the church's pulpit one Sunday in August of 1706. Long repentant Ann wrote that she had "just grounds and good reason to believe they [the accused and executed] were innocent persons; and that it was a great delusion of Satan that deceived me in that sad time . . . I did it not out of any anger, malice, or ill evil." The Reverend Mr. Green's mild manner served as a balm to heal the deep divisions within the parish and neighborhood. In the background at 199 Hobart Street is the 17th-century Ingersoll Tavern (one of three in the village then), owned by church deacon Nathaniel Ingersoll. Some accused witches were examined there, and after the "novelty" of the event, townspeople enjoyed cider and or beer at the tavern, which was remodeled in 1753, the year after Salem Village was renamed Danvers.

Regni *ANNÆ* Reginæ Decimo.

Province of the
Maſſachuſetts-Bay.

AN ACT,

Made and Paſſed by the Great and General Court. or
Aſſembly of Her Majeſty's Province of the Maſſachuſetts-
Bay in **New-England**, Held at **Boſton** the 17th
Day of **October**, 1 7 1 1.   *Nat Lambert Salen*

                                    Jany 28ᵗʰ 1808

An Act to Reverſe the Attainders of *George Burroughs* and others for Witchcraft.

FOR ASMUCH *as in the Year of our Lord One Thouſand*
Six Hundred Ninety Two, Several Towns within this Pro-
vince were Infeſted with a horrible Witchcraft or Poſſeſſion
of Devils ; And at a Special Court of Oyer and Terminer
holden at Salem, *in the County of* Eſſex *in the ſame Year*
One Thouſand Six Hundred Ninety Two, George Burroughs *of Wells,*
John Procter, George Jacob, John Willard, Giles Core, *and*
his Wife, Rebecca Nurſe, *and* Sarah Good, *all of* Salem *aforeſaid* :
Elizabeth How, *of* Ipſwich, Mary Eaſtey, Sarah Wild *and* Abigail Hobbs *all of* Topsfield : Samuel Wardell, Mary Parker,
Martha Carrier, Abigail Falkner, Anne Foſter, Rebecca Eames,
Mary Poſt, *and* Mary Lacey, *all of* Andover : Mary Bradbury
of Salisbury : *and* Dorcas Hoar *of* Beverly ; *Were ſeverally In-*
dicted, Convicted and Attained of Witchcraft, and ſome of them put
to Death, Others lying ſtill under the like Sentence of the ſaid Court,
and liable to have the ſame Executed upon them.
    A   **The**

AN ACT TO REVERSE THE ATTAINDERS OF GEORGE BURROUGHS AND OTHERS FOR WITCHCRAFT (OCTOBER 17, 1711). Queen Anne's "Great and General Court . . . Province of the Massachusetts-Bay" apportioned "578 pounds, 12 shillings" as financial compensation for the relief of victims' "relatives [who] were imprisoned, impaired, and blasted in their reputations and estates," stated Philip English two years beforehand. On August 28, 1957, the same state court passed a resolve, signed by Gov. Foster Furcolo, to free the descendants of the accused and executed from the inherited "guilt and shame" associated with the witchcraft trials. Ann Pudeator, who was hanged as a witch on September 22, 1692, was one of the last victims to be so pardoned 265 years later.

Two

WITCHCRAFT MEMORIALS

THE SALEM VILLAGE WITCHCRAFT VICTIMS' MEMORIAL, 176 HOBART STREET, DANVERS (1992 PHOTOGRAPH). Two freestanding granite sculptures, imposing in their solidity and simplicity, were erected on town-owned land opposite the site of the first meetinghouse "in memory of those innocents who died during the Salem Village witchcraft hysteria of 1692." Richard B. Trask, town archivist and chairman of the Tercentennial Committee, designed the pulpit with a Bible on the carved box and flanking iron chains, while project architect and committee member Robert D. Farley designed the three-section enveloping wall and the surrounding concrete plaza. Puritan religious iconography was a concern of the third designer, committee member Marjorie C. Wetzel. On the day of dedication, May 9, 1992, townspeople and guests sat in awe under a large tent, or stood nearby, as a black pall was removed to reveal the memorial "to serve as a vital and long-needed reminder of the dangers of prejudice, intolerance, and fear." (Courtesy Robert D. Farley.)

41

REBECCA NURSE MEMORIAL IN NURSE BURIAL GROUND, 149 PINE STREET (C. 1892 PHOTOGRAPH BY FRANK COUSINS). The first and still the most impressive monument erected to a single victim of the witchcraft delusion is the Quincy and Rockport granite shaft to honor one of the first and certainly the most memorable person accused. Rebecca Nurse was so revered by most of her neighbors that 40 signed a document defending her blameless character, to be read at her trial; those names are on a nearby stone. The account of Goody Nurse's beatific demeanor, trial, and execution—her frail body was thrown into a crevasse, but according to family legend, it was secretly removed that night by relatives and buried somewhere under pine trees on the family farm—inspired poet John Greenleaf Whittier (1807–1892), then a Danvers resident, to compose a short poem that was engraved on one of the polished sides of the impressive monument, which is 8.5 feet high. (Courtesy Schier Collection.)

The Commonwealth of Massachusetts

A Proclamation

By His Excellency
GOVERNOR WILLIAM F. WELD
1992

WHEREAS: In 1692, over 150 inhabitants of Massachusetts were arrested and imprisoned for the perceived crime of witchcraft; and

WHEREAS: In ensuing legal action, nineteen women and men were executed by hanging, while one man was tortured to death and at least five died as a result of their incarceration; and

WHEREAS: Those who were executed had refused to confess to something they knew they did not do, even when it became evident that confessed witches were spared their lives; and

WHEREAS: The courage and steadfastness of these condemned persons adhering to truth when the legal, clerical and political institutions failed them, is worthy of remembrance and commemoration; and

WHEREAS: It is also fitting that on this, the 300th anniversary of the Salem Village witchcraft delusion, we are reminded that intolerance and "witch hunts" are not necessarily merely incidents of the distant past but can still occur in numerous forms and must be confronted and avoided by each new generation; and

WHEREAS: In commemoration of the anniversary of the first witchcraft related death on May 10th, 1692 the Town of Danvers will dedicate the Witchcraft Victims' Memorial on May 9th, 1992;

NOW, THEREFORE, I, WILLIAM F. WELD, Governor of the Commonwealth of Massachusetts, do hereby honor

THE SALEM VILLAGE WITCHCRAFT VICTIMS

and urge the citizens of the Commonwealth to take cognizance of this event and participate fittingly in its observance.

Given at the Executive Chamber in Boston, this first day of May, in the year one thousand nine hundred and ninety-two, and in the year of the Independence of the United States of America, the two hundred and sixteenth.

William F. Weld
WILLIAM F. WELD

By His Excellency the Governor

Michael J. Connolly
MICHAEL J. CONNOLLY
Secretary of the Commonwealth

GOD SAVE THE COMMONWEALTH OF MASSACHUSETTS

A PROCLAMATION BY GOV. WILLIAM F. WELD TO HONOR "THE SALEM VILLAGE WITCHCRAFT VICTIMS" (MAY 1, 1992).

DEDICATION OF THE
SALEM VILLAGE
WITCHCRAFT VICTIMS' MEMORIAL

176 Hobart Street
Danvers, Massachusetts

May 9, 1992, 2:00 p.m.

The Salem Village Witchcraft Tercentennial Committee
of the Town of Danvers

A PROGRAM FOR THE DEDICATION OF THE SALEM VILLAGE WITCHCRAFT VICTIMS' MEMORIAL (MAY 9, 1992). An overcast day turned miraculously sunny for the approximately 3,000 people who attended the commemorative exercises, which included relevant remarks, period music, and the tolling of local church bells. Many had their programs stamped and hand-canceled by a representative of the United States Post Office with the especially designed 300th anniversary stamp.

A TOUCHING CEREMONY (MAY 9, 1992). Attired simply in black for presenting "John Willard Remembers," the Rev. Dr. Peter Wilfred Stine, pastor of the First Baptist Church of Danvers, lovingly and silently passes his hand over carved names, including Willard's, on the Salem Village Witchcraft Memorial at the dedication. Professor Stine of Gordon College in Wenham recited the Lord's Prayer before the college choir sang two 18th-century musical selections by William Billings. (Courtesy the Reverend Mr. Stine.)

REMEMBERING 1692 (JULY 19, 1992). Costumed interpreters Robert and Elaine Dow prepare to give a dramatic reading of court records as part of "a commemorative program on the occasion of the 300th anniversary of the execution of five Essex County women" on the grounds of the Nurse Homestead. The historic event began with a long drum roll, followed by various remarks, including those of Victor R. Pisano, the screenwriter and producer of the docu-drama *Three Sovereigns for Sarah*. The Gloucester Hornpipe and Clog Society presented a stirring musical selection based on the life and death of Susannah Martin.

A WREATH-LAYING CEREMONY AT THE NURSE BURIAL GROUND (JULY 19, 1992). More than 300 interested people witnessed the wreath-laying and floral tributes to the 5 executed women and the 40 individuals who bravely petitioned to spare the life of Rebecca Nurse. After the solemn afternoon ceremony guests enjoyed meeting each other at the reception, where light refreshments were served.

THE GRAVESTONE OF GEORGE JACOBS SR., NURSE BURIAL GROUND. The purported remains of Mr. Jacobs were placed in a 17th-century-style peaked pine coffin during a solemn ceremony on Sunday morning, August 2, 1992. At his trial, the witchcraft victim exclaimed, "You tax me for a wizard, you may as well tax me for a buzzard. I have done no harm." He was convicted on one count because he failed to correctly repeat the Lord's Prayer (a good indication of a non-practicing Puritan Christian). Jacobs also emphatically stated, "Well burn me, or hang me, I will stand in the truth of Christ, I know nothing of it [witchcraft]."

THE MEMORIAL TO WILMOT REDD, OLD BURIAL HILL, MARBLEHEAD. An hourglass is featured on the commemorative gravestone of Marblehead's only accused and executed "innocent victim," Wilmot "Mammy" Redd. The middle-aged fisherman's wife lived near the other side of Redd's Pond, prompting this memorial to be erected in 1998. When questioned about her involvement in malevolent deeds, she retorted, "I know nothing of it."

THE MEMORIAL TO JOHN PROCTOR SR., LOWELL STREET AT THE CORNER OF SUMMIT STREET, PEABODY. Situated within view of the family farmhouse at 348 Lowell Street, this memorial commemorates the life of the Salem Farmes licensed tavern keeper, who along with his wife, Elizabeth, was accused of witchcraft. She was spared because she was with child, but John, who was about 60 years of age, was executed on August 19. While in prison, he wrote a letter to some learned Boston gentlemen hoping that the trials could be transferred there with more tolerant magistrates present.

THE MEMORIAL TO SUSANNAH MARTIN, AT THE CUL DE SAC ON MARTIN ROAD NORTH IN AMESBURY, OFF ROUTE E110. At her trial, the widow Martin stated, "Amen. Amen. A false tongue will never make a guilty person." The bronze plaque with stone was dedicated in 1894, and states "Here stood the house of / Susannah Martin / an honest, hardworking / Christian woman/ Accused as a witch, Tried, and executed at Salem, July 19, 1692. A Martyr of Superstition."

47

THE EVOLUTION OF TWO DREAMS (1987 PHOTOGRAPH). The almost 30-year passion of local resident Peter M. McSwiggin (right), shown here with sculptor Yiannis Stefanakis in studio space at the East India Mall in Salem, was planned to be completed in time for the tercentenary. Spearheaded by McSwiggin, The Sons and Daughters of the Victims of Colonial Witch Trials selected the sculptor's prototype clay model, which was based on the film *Three Sovereigns for Sarah*. However, the life-size plaster model was not cast in bronze because it lacked total funding, a permanent home, and was not officially sanctioned by the city; it may now be seen at the Salem Wax Museum of Witches & Seafarers, where it overlooks the Old Burying Point. (Courtesy Peter M. McSwiggin.)

THE SALEM WITCH TRIALS MEMORIAL. A 6,000-square-foot temporary park—flanked by the Old Burying Point (the Charter Street Cemetery), the Peabody Essex Museum's late-17th-century Samuel Pickman House and its gardens, and the parking lot for the 12-story Salem Housing Authority—was transformed into the city's first permanent witchcraft memorial. Patricia MacLeod, chairman of the Salem Witch Trials Memorial committee, spearheaded the project. This design, by architect James Cutler and artist Maggie Smith of Winslow, Washington, was chosen from 246 entries. Stepped granite blocks arranged in a U-shaped design incorporate 20 cantilevered memorial slabs, each of which has the carved name and execution date of a witchcraft victim. There is a separate row of stepped granite blocks, one of which bears the names of donors below the carved inscription "this memorial is dedicated to the enduring lessons of human rights and tolerance learned from the Salem Witch Trials of 1692." The memorial has won several awards, including the A.I.A. honor award for excellence in design in 1993.

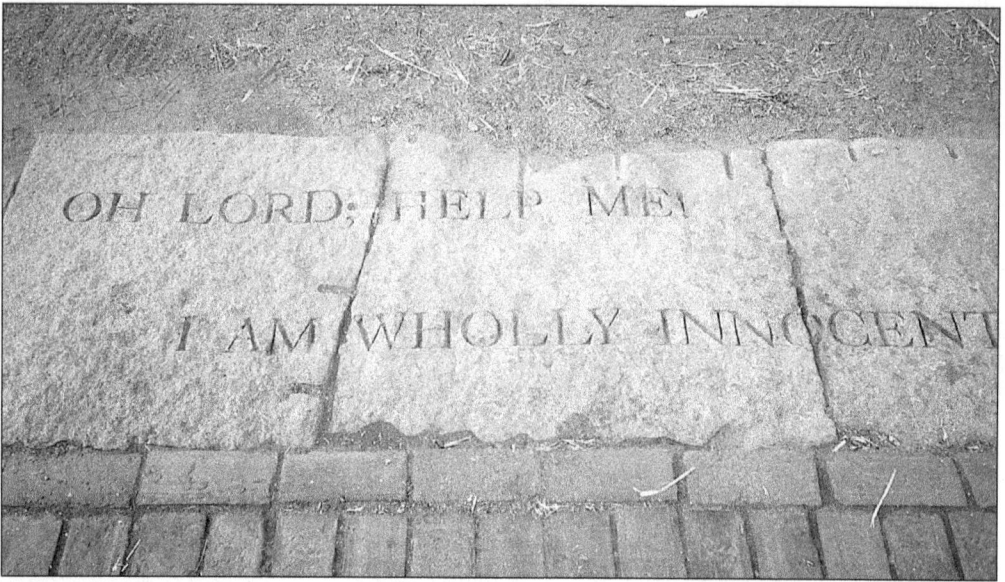

THE WALKWAY ENTRANCE TO THE SALEM WITCH TRIALS MEMORIAL. An appropriate letter style was chosen for the overall design, here with an incomplete, or truncated, sentence, which relates to a victim's voice being silenced in the courtroom and at Gallows Hill. The six thorny black locust trees centering the open, contemplative memorial, which are underlit in the evening, symbolize the type of trees many historians believe were used in the executions.

" *Let them think what they will . . . I dare not tell a lie if it would save my life.* "

Susannah Martin
Hanged July 19, 1692

SALEM WITCH TRIALS

TERCENTENARY

MEMORIAL DEDICATION
Wednesday, August 5, 1992

THE SALEM WITCH TRIALS TERCENTENARY MEMORIAL DEDICATION (AUGUST 5, 1992). Interest in the witchcraft episode first peaked in 1892, the bicentennial year. At an Essex Institute lecture, Salem Mayor Robert Rantoul remarked, "History imparts on us . . . a delicate and difficult task. We are here to commemorate something we would willingly forget. The witchcraft horror—the terrible frenzy which overtook our ancestors two centuries ago—is a chapter in our local annals which I for one would make haste to blot out forever if I had it in my power to do so."

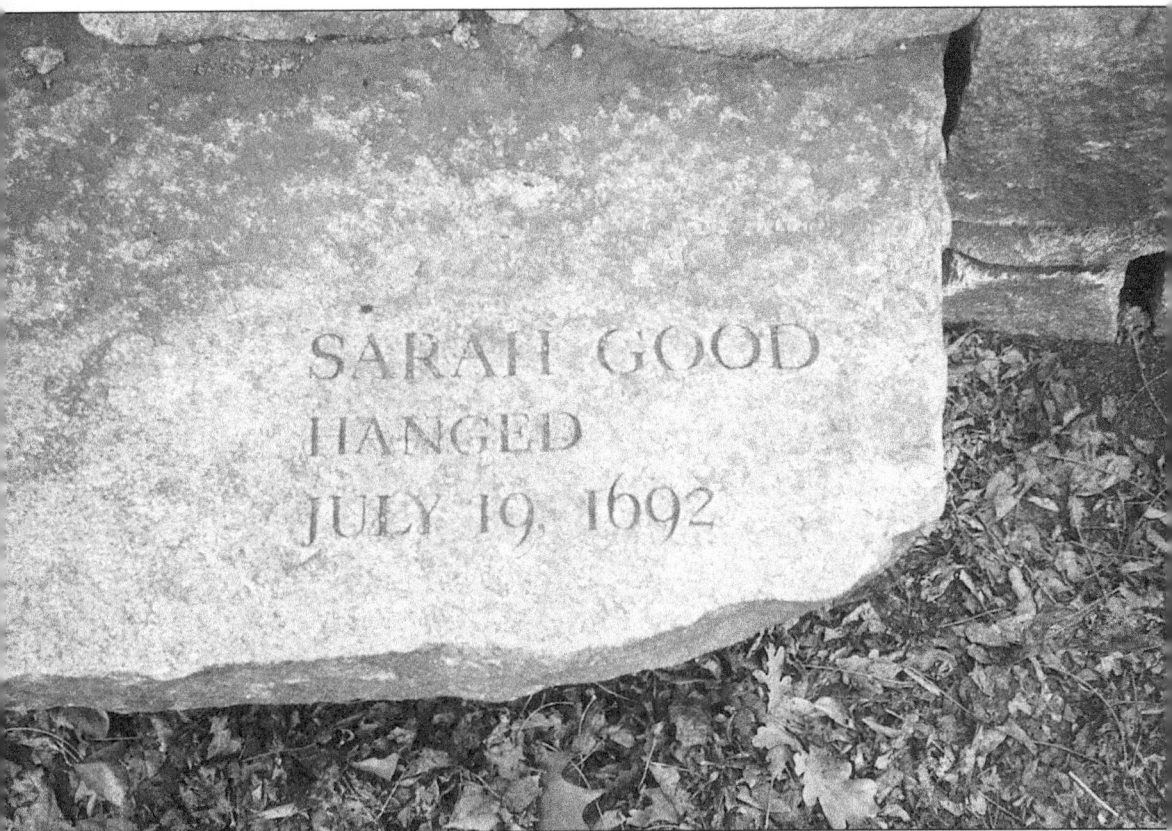

THE MEMORIAL TO SARAH GOOD, SALEM WITCH TRIALS MEMORIAL. The last words of pipe-smoking, condemned witch Sarah Good inspired Salem-born author Nathaniel Hawthorne to write *The House of the Seven Gables*. While waiting for the noose to be tightened around her neck on Gallows Hill, Goody Good was taunted by Rev. Nicholas Noyes, who exclaimed that she was a witch. She retorted, "You are a lyer; I am no more a Witch than you are a Wizard, and if you take away my Life, God will give you Blood to drink." The corpulent Noyes later died of a hemorrhage, fulfilling the prophecy.

IN MEMORY OF GEORGE BURROUGHS (1998 ACRYLIC PAINTING BY WENDY SNOW-LANG). The Salem illustrator included a Bible to represent the ministry of the Reverend Mr. Burroughs, a black cat as the typical witch's familiar, and a white rose to depict the many floral offerings left at the Salem Witch Trials Memorial. Rev. George Burroughs was the second minister to the flock in Salem Village. While there, his specter informed Ann Putnam Sr. that he had murdered his first two wives; that he had caused the conversion of many villagers to witchcraft; and that he had instigated the murders of militiamen in the colony. Although described as "a little man," nine villagers accused Burroughs "for extraordinary Lifting, and such feats of Strength, as could not be done without a Diabolical Assistance." His execution was almost halted by his impeccable recitation of the Lord's Prayer; when the crowd became uneasy, Cotton Mather, while on horseback, told them that the devil often appeared as an Angel of Light. According to legend, a hasty burial failed to cover part of the minister's earthly body. (Courtesy of the artist.)

Three

MUSEUMS AND
HISTORIC SITES

A SALEM WITCHCRAFT TRAIL MAP (1998). The parking garage opposite the National Park Service Visitors' Center on New Liberty Street is the recommended starting point for the walkable witchcraft trail. A number of the sites are seen on guided tours, which is an informative way to learn about Salem's other historical attractions. Images included in this chapter are numbered to correspond with the map, either with a house to indicate a museum, or a square for a site. The images not shown are as follows: 1.] St. Peter's Church, 24 St. Peter Street; 2.] The site of Giles Cory's execution, Howard Street Cemetery; 5.] The site of the Reverend Nicholas Noyes House, corner of Washington and Lynde Streets; 14.] The site of the Judge Bartholomew Gedney House, southeast corner of Summer and Broad Streets; and 22.] The site of the Ann Pudeator House, near corner of Washington Square North and Winter Street.

[3] THE SITE OF THE OLD WITCH GAOL, 4 FEDERAL STREET (C. 1892 PHOTOGRAPH BY FRANK COUSINS). The third gaol (jail) in Salem was constructed in 1684 of massive oak beams near the intersection of St. Peter Street, which was then known as Prison Lane. Enlarged during the late 18th century, it served as a jail until 1813, when the large granite jail nearby was completed (construction on it had begun in 1811). Abner Cheney Goodell purchased the house in 1863. In 1935 his grandson, Alfred Putnam Goodell, and his wife began to run it as a tourist attraction. Visitors toured the dungeon, read an original unpaid bill for a witch's upkeep, listened to lectures by guides, and saw other "interesting exhibits." (Courtesy Schier Collection.)

Old Witch Gaol

Built 1684
Abandoned 1813
Razed 1956

In 1692, During The
Salem Witch Trials,
Many Of The Accused
Were Imprisoned Here.

[6] THE OLD WITCH GAOL PLAQUE, APPROXIMATELY AT THE LOCATION OF 4 FEDERAL STREET. The New England Telephone Company razed the house that contained the jail in 1956 for the construction of a new office. Local historian and genealogist Edward Windsor Carberg was instrumental in having this bronze plaque made to replace the original one, which is now on the exterior of the Witch Dungeon Museum.

[4] THE SITE OF THE BRIDGET BISHOP HOUSE, LYCEUM HALL, 43 CHURCH STREET (C. 1892 PHOTOGRAPH BY FRANK COUSINS). No artistic rendering of Bishop's dwelling exists. It was located on the street named for the first wood-framed edifice of St. Peter's Church, the granite replacement of which is visible here in the distance. On February 12, 1877, Lyceum Hall became a historically significant structure when Alexander Graham Bell demonstrated his invention of the telephone by calling his assistant, Thomas Watson, at their laboratory on Exeter Street in Boston. The present Colonial Revival brick building was constructed a few years after the photograph was taken. (Courtesy Schier Collection.)

[3 AND 11] THE OLD WITCH JAIL AND DUNGEON AND THE OLD WITCH HOUSE (C. 1940 HANDBILL). The enticing information and illustration of a witch flying over Salem buildings caught the attention of many tourists in the "Witch City," most of whom visited these early sites, which were open to the public. Unlike her grandfather, George Jacobs Sr., Margaret Jacobs was a confessed witch, who in 1692 stated that ". . . being closely confined in Salem jail, for the crime of witchcraft, which . . . I am altogether innocent of . . . I should be put down into the dungeon [if I did not confess], and would be hanged . . ."

Don't Miss Seeing the

OLD WITCH JAIL AND DUNGEON
One of New England's Most Historical Buildings
Open to the Public Every Day 9 to 6 P. M.
Evenings by Appointment
Free Parking Space
Built 1684 — Witchcraft Jail 1692
Discontinued as Jail 1813
4 FEDERAL ST.   SALEM, MASS.
Residence Phone Salem 2948-R

OLD WITCH HOUSE
COR. NORTH & ESSEX STS.
Examinations of those accused of
WITCHCRAFT took place here.
An Original Witch Lamp.
Complete line of Authentic Antique Furniture,
Glass Ware, Clocks and China For Sale.
Collectors' Paradise.
Open Every Week Day 10 A. M. to 5:30 P. M.
A. GRACE ATKINSON, Prop.
(Over)

PRINTED BY UNION LABOR

[6] THE COURTHOUSE AND THE GILES CORY PLAQUE, 70 WASHINGTON STREET. This early-20th-century descriptive bronze plaque is located to the left of the Masonic Temple's main entrance.

[7 AND 8] TOWN HOUSE SQUARE, INTERSECTION OF ESSEX AND WASHINGTON STREETS (C. 1870S STEREOPTICON VIEW). This imposing Greek Revival brick-and-stone building is on the site of the First Church [7], where Rebecca Nurse was excommunicated by Rev. John Higginson and his assistant, Rev. Nicholas Noyes, at the afternoon meeting on July 3, 1692. It is interesting to note that the present building later became Daniel Low & Co., and was the first store in Salem to begin selling witchcraft souvenirs during the last decade of the 19th century. Judge John Hathorne's 17th-century dwelling was on the site of the three-story Italiante structure at 114 Washington Street [8]. (Courtesy Theriault Collection.)

[9] THE SITE OF THE SHERIFF GEORGE CORWIN HOUSE, 148 WASHINGTON STREET. When the 31-year-old "Gentleman High Sheriff of the County of Essex" died prematurely in 1697, his corpse was threatened to be seized by accused witch Philip English, who later claimed he was "Embezeled" by the sheriff. Corwin's cadaver was buried temporarily on his property until English's suit of debt was paid. Housewright Samuel Luscomb Jr. has recently been credited as the designer of this early Federal-style brick mansion, built for Joshua Ward between 1784 and 1788.

[10] **WITCH DUNGEON MUSEUM, 16 LYNDE STREET.** Situated opposite Sewall Street (named for the Stephen Sewall House, which was once located on the present site of the YMCA at the other end of the street), the Witch Dungeon Museum is housed in the former First Church of Christ Scientist in Salem. Several years after being deconsecrated, the Gothic-style church, which was built in 1897, was acquired and partially converted into a museum, opening to the public in 1979. An oak timber from the original Witch Gaol is on view in the dungeon section of the establishment.

[10] **ACCUSED OF WITCHCRAFT, WITCH DUNGEON MUSEUM.** Guided tours of the museum begin in the former sanctuary, where professional actresses in repertory reenact the courtroom trials of several different women who had been accused of practicing witchcraft. Elizabeth Proctor, John's wife (left), is visibly shaken by her afflicted servant, Mary Warren, who claims to see a yellow bird as her pregnant mistress's specter. Visitors then follow a narrator into the dank basement to view various tableaux and cell scenes as part of the "unique educational experience with a chill or two."

[11] THE OLD WITCH HOUSE, 310 1/2 ESSEX STREET, SALEM (PRE-1868 PHOTOGRAPH). Judge Jonathan Corwin's former home, built after 1642, was remodeled in 1746 by the widow of his grandson from a gabled-roofed dwelling to one that featured a gambrel roof, without the projecting porch. It is now the only remaining 17th-century house in Salem directly connected to the witch trials. When photographed, a town pump and a gas-lighted street lantern gave the residence added ambiance with its mysteriously shuttered second-floor windows and paired fan-shaped rose trellises. (Courtesy Schier Collection.)

[11] THE OLD WITCH HOUSE MAIN ENTRANCE (C. 1910 POSTCARD PUBLISHED BY AMERICAN ART POST CARD CO., BOSTON, MA). Different signs adjacent to the entrance of the house around this period included "Old Chimney, Fireplace and Trial Room/Walk Through Drug Store/Visitors Welcome," "Fine Antiques on Sale," and "Ye Old Witch House Antiques Bought and Sold." In 1901, James C. Casey advertised in the city directory that he sold "Antique Furniture, Historic Ware and Colonial Goods" at the above address. As early as the 1860s, William T. Servey fabricated "parasols and sunshades . . . on order, covered, lined, ruffled, and bugled [trimmed with glass beads] in every style." (Courtesy Theriault Collection.)

[11] UPTON & FRISBEE, PHARMACISTS (C. 1900 STEREOPTICON VIEW). George P. Farrington added a one-story projecting apothecary shop to the Jonathan Corwin House around 1856. In 1884, when William E. Luscomb became a partner, the business was renamed Farrington & Luscomb; it was renamed again when it was purchased by Jesse F. Upton and Frank H. Frisbee, who continued to serve the carriage trade and walk-ins between 1895 and 1940. The shaped sign between the attic windows incorrectly associates banished First Church minister Roger Williams with the "Witch House." (Courtesy Theriault Collection.)

[11] THE OLD WITCH HOUSE (C. 1950S POSTCARD PUBLISHED BY COLOURPICTURE, BOSTON, MA). Preservation and restoration of the post-1642 structure was begun in 1945 by Historic Salem, Inc., when it was threatened by the widening of North Street; it was moved in a sling back from Essex Street by about 35 feet. Restored by Boston architect Gordon Robb along with consulting architect Frank Chouteau Brown, the title to the property was transferred to the city of Salem one year after it opened to the public on Memorial Day weekend in 1947. (Courtesy Schier Collection.)

[11] THE HALL OF THE WITCH HOUSE (C. 1970 POSTCARD PUBLISHED BY BROMLEY & CO., BOSTON, MA). In England and New England the best room in early dwellings was referred to as the "hall." Diurnal and nocturnal activities occurred in this large area; people cooked in the spacious fireplace with its various accouterments, and slept here, often in lumpy press beds, which could be pressed against the wall when not in use. Closets were not in vogue then, so clothing was stored in press or court cupboards, or in simple six-board chests, such as the one holding a man's hat and a circular pierced-tin foot warmer. (Courtesy Theriault Collection.)

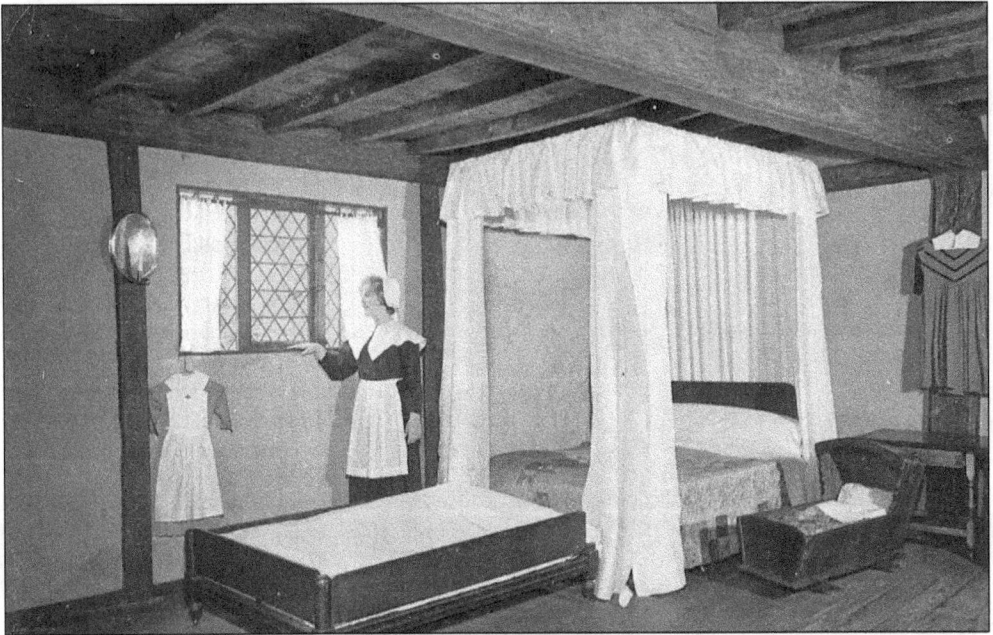

[11] THE WEST BEDCHAMBER OF THE WITCH HOUSE (C. 1970 POSTCARD PUBLISHED BY BROMLEY & COMPANY). A costumed high school docent poses by a casement window next to the trundle bed (with added sides) that has been pulled from beneath the four-poster bedstead, dressed in stark, white cotton for the summer season. (Courtesy Theriault Collection.)

61

GALLOWS OR "WITCH HILL" (C. 1885 PEN-AND-INK DRAWING IN *SOUVENIR OF SALEM, MASS.*). Despite many suggestions advocating a monument, some as early as 1828, no monument or memorial has been erected on the city's most infamous hill. Plots of land had been built upon during the mid- to late 19th century, and from 1890 to 1962 the summit was the setting for the annual Fourth of July bonfire, when a towering stack of grease-soaked wooden barrels from nearby factories could be seen blazing for hours in adjacent cities. A water tower has dominated the historic site since then. (Courtesy Schier Collection.)

[12] THE SITE OF THE STEPHEN SEWALL HOUSE, CORNER OF ESSEX AND SEWALL STREETS (C. 1895 PHOTOGRAPH). A Federal-period brick townhouse was built on the site of the 17th-century residence of Judge Samuel Sewall's brother Stephen, who served as clerk of the Court of Oyer and Terminer. Sometime during the middle of March in 1692, Rev. Samuel Parris sent his impressionable daughter, Betty, to live with the Sewalls to keep her away from further interactions with the "afflicted children." (Courtesy Theriault Collection.)

[13] THE ENTRANCE TO THE BROAD STREET CEMETERY (1998 PEN-AND-INK DRAWING BY RACKET SHREVE). Artistic license was used by the Chestnut Street, Salem, artist when incorporating the winged death-head on the gravestone near the Winthrop Street entrance to the city's second oldest cemetery. The earliest extant slate gravestone with a similar motif in the tympanum is that of Mary Lamburt, the wife of Daniel Lamburt, who died in August of 1693. The latest is that of Mrs. Mary Smith, consort of Capt. Hugh Smith, who departed this life in 1782. Sheriff George Corwin's remains lie with relatives in the southwest section of the cemetery, marked by a small white marble obelisk. The most unusual tomb is that of Benjamin Goodhue, Esq., who died in 1789. Located adjacent to the fenced-in Plummer family lot near the Summer Street side of the final resting place, Mr. Goodhue's oval granite tomb has a conforming "table-stone" slate top with the remains of a vandalized, or weather-beaten, skull at the base of the raised shield. (Courtesy Martha Shreve.)

[15] THE ENTRANCE TO THE SALEM WAX MUSEUM OF WITCHES & SEAFARERS, 288 DERBY STREET. Greeting visitors to the multi-sensory exhibition is a clerically garbed figure to represent Rev. Samuel Parris. A total of 53 wax figures, in unique scenes relating to the witchcraft hysteria and the exploits of seafarers, are included in the 25 minute theater-in-the-round presentation. Children and adults can participate in gravestone rubbing (no longer permitted in Salem cemeteries), inspect a dungeon, and see a courtroom scene of the past. The exterior deck overlooks the Old Burying Point with the gravestone of Judge Hathorne in the immediate area.

[15] A WAX FIGURE REPRESENTING GILES CORY, SALEM WAX MUSEUM OF WITCHES & SEAFARERS. Usually depicted in a prostrate position, Giles Cory of Salem Farmes stands to greet visitors when they enter the lively presentation. The realistic wax figures were crafted in St. Augustine, Florida, and in London, England.

[17] THE OLD BURYING POINT AND DR. GRIMSHAW'S HOUSE, 53 CHARTER STREET (C. 1888 ETCHING BY GEORGE M. WHITE). A wooden sign inside Salem's first cemetery lists some of the names of important local citizens interred therein, and a bronze tablet mounted on granite indicates where their gravestones are located. The venerable cemetery has an imposing granite retaining wall along Derby Street that kept the South River at bay before it was reduced in width and depth. Sophia Peabody, Nathaniel Hawthorne's fiancée, resided with her family in the c. 1770 dwelling directly abutting the cemetery.

[17] THE TOMBSTONE OF COL. JOHN HATHORNE, THE WITCH JUDGE, OLD BURYING POINT, CHARTER STREET (1905 POSTCARD PUBLISHED BY THE ROTOGRAPH COMPANY, NEW YORK CITY). In order to disassociate himself from his "witch judge" ancestor, Salem-born author Nathaniel Hawthorne added a "w" to the family surname. Hawthorne wrote in *The Scarlet Letter* (1850) that his magisterial ancestor "made himself so conspicuous in the martyrdom of the witches, that their blood may fairly be said to have left a stain upon him." (CourtesySchier Collection.)

[17] TIMOTHY LINDALL'S GRAVESTONE, OLD BURYING POINT, CHARTER STREET (C. 1892 PHOTOGRAPH BY FRANK COUSINS). "Sanctorum Memoria Sit Beata" ("May the memory of the saints be blessed") is the Latin motto below the realistic winged head (which may be a portrait of the deceased) on this distinctively carved slate gravestone. Father Time, balancing an hourglass on his head while holding a scythe, and a well-delineated skeleton flank the epitaph. Although Timothy Lindall, Philip English, and three other inhabitants of Salem Town had been elected to the office of selectmen in March of 1692, they were voted out of office in July at the height of the hysteria. (Courtesy Schier Collection.)

[17] THE GRAVESTONE OF MARY CORRY [SIC], OLD BURYING POINT, CHARTER STREET (C. 1892 PHOTOGRAPH BY FRANK COUSINS). The elements have taken their unrelenting toll, unfortunately, on the simple sandstone grave marker of Mary, Giles Cory's first wife. (Courtesy Schier Collection.)

[18] SALEM'S MUSEUM OF MYTHS AND MONSTERS, PICKERING WHARF. "Professor Nightmare" (a.k.a. John Denley), the founder of Boneyard Productions, has fabricated at least 15 haunted houses around the country. A ghoulish guide beckons visitors to follow him through the Salem fright site, which has hi-tech FX and detailed theatrical sets. The museum section of "Terror on the Wharf" (a name change during the month of October) features a reproduction of Frankenstein's head used in the first horror film that featured Mary Shelley's creation, and a Freddie Krueger mask made for *Nightmare on Elm Street V*. (Courtesy John Denley.)

[19] THE SITE OF THOMAS BEADLE'S TAVERN, 65 ESSEX STREET (C. 1892 PHOTOGRAPH BY FRANK COUSINS). Two groups of Phillips School students stand near the mansard-roofed house, which was built during the Victorian period on the site of Beadle's Tavern, where some pre-trial examinations were held. Located three buildings to the right, at 71 Essex Street, is the *c.* 1672 Narbonne House, whose occupants in 1692 were probably witnesses to some of the events of that horrific year. (Courtesy Schier Collection.)

[20] THE PHILLIPS LIBRARY OF THE PEABODY ESSEX MUSEUM, 132 ESSEX STREET (C. 1892 PHOTOGRAPH BY FRANK COUSINS). Since its founding in 1848 with the merger of two earlier societies, the former Essex Institute (now the Peabody Essex Museum) has been the major repository for the material culture of Essex County's rich past. The John Tucker Daland House (right), built in the Italianate style in 1851–52, contains some of the library's offices; the five-story brick fireproof addition at the rear of the building holds on its miles of shelves more than 500 original documents and hundreds of volumes relating to witchcraft. Plummer Hall's complimentary brick-and-brownstone façade (left), constructed in 1856–57 for the Salem Athenaeum, is the location of the library's remodeled reading rooms on the second floor. Galleries off the first floor's grand entrance have held several interpretive witchcraft exhibitions since 1971. (Courtesy Schier Collection.)

[20] THE ENTRANCE TO THE PHILLIPS LIBRARY, 132 ESSEX STREET. The very popular exhibitions "Days of the Dead: The Arts of Los Muertos" and "The Real Witchcraft Papers" drew an estimated 8,000 visitors during Haunted Happenings in 1998. Historic houses on the museum's campus are open on weekends during the Hallowe'en season for "Eerie Events," when costumed guides relate gripping ghost stories in the moonlit gardens.

Celebrating
17th century Salem
at the Essex Institute

two special exhibitions
SALEM WITCHES: MYTH AND REALITY
now through September 30, 1979

350th ANNIVERSARY OF THE GATHERING OF THE FIRST CHURCH, SALEM, 1629-1979
during July and August

Essex Institute
132 Essex Street
Salem, Massachusetts 01970
744-3390

[20] AN EXHIBITION POSTER (1979). These commemorative exhibitions were held in the former McCarthy Gallery, located in the rear hallway of the institute's 1907 Renaissance Revival connecting section. Mercy Short of Boston, while recovering from "abominable witchcrafts" in the home of Rev. Cotton Mather, told him that the devil was "a witch no taller than an ordinary Walkingstaff; he was not of a Negro, but of a Tawney, or an Indian color; hee wore an high-crowned Hat with strait Hair and had one Cloven Foot."

[20] A "DAYS OF JUDGMENT" COMMEMORATIVE POSTER (1992). North Shore resident Olivia Parker, an internationally recognized artist and photographer, created and donated a four-color collage for the important tercentenary exhibition "Days of Judgment: The Salem Witch Trials of 1692," held at the Essex Institute from June 13 to November 29, 1992. Late-17th-century Puritan secular and non-secular (diabolical) iconography overlap in the intriguing design, and were also interwoven in the topical fall lecture series "Belief/Bigotry: Witchcraft and Witch Hunts, 1692–1992," presented by four distinguished speakers—Margot Adler, Laurie Cabot, John Demos, and David Hall. (Courtesy of the artist.)

[20] THE REAL WITCHCRAFT PAPERS, THE PHILLIPS LIBRARY. The slat, or ladderback, Great Chair, originally owned by Mary English, is the most important piece of furniture in the collection, with a pedigree dating to 1692. It was acquired by Rev. Dr. William Bentley, who replaced the rush seat with a wooden one, had the chair painted a dark green, and had an artist paint the following historical information on the three shaped slats: "It shall be told of her" (top slat front), and "1692/M,, English./Ap:22" (rear slats). Mary's husband, Philip English, owned the ivory-topped wooden cane in the adjacent plexiglass case.

[20] THE REAL WITCHCRAFT PAPERS, THE PHILLIPS LIBRARY. The free-standing wooden cane in the other plexiglass case was used by George Jacobs Sr, depicted in the painting on the gallery (see p. 30). John Proctor Sr. owned the brass sundial, made in England in 1644, displayed in the small case. Some other authentic artifacts often on exhibit include an oil portrait of Judge Samuel Sewall by John Smibert; a decorative linen sampler made by Mary Hollingsworth, c. 1665 (before she married Philip English); and the seal from a green glass bottle bearing the owner's name "Philip English."

[20] THE ARREST WARRANT FOR ALICE PARKER AND ANN PUDEATOR, MAY 12, 1692 (C. 1892 PHOTOGRAPH BY FRANK COUSINS). An arrest warrant usually included the phrase "for high suspition [sic] of sundry acts of witchcraft . . ." Parker and Pudeator were arrested on May 12 and incarcerated in jail for four months preceding their trials. Original Salem-related witchcraft documents now exceed 850 in number and are in various collections. The largest number, well over 500, were contained in large books along with the aforementioned "witch pins" in the Essex County Superior Court in Salem. In 1980, this important collection was placed on permanent deposit with the former Essex Institute, and they were archivally restored. (Collection Peabody Essex Museum.)

[20] DR. WILLIAM BENTLEY (1759–1819, OIL PAINTING ON CANVAS BY JAMES FROTHINGHAM, 1786–1864). The highly respected bachelor minister of the East Church was an antiquarian and linguist who kept a well-documented diary while he boarded with the Crowninshield family at 106 Essex Street for 28 years. On October 1, 1798, Bentley wrote "Found that the notions of *Witchcraft* & the belief of the facts of 1692 were not eradicated." Five years earlier the eminent ecclesiastical scholar devoted several pages to the history of Philip and Mary English, noting "Philip English gave the Land where the English Church [St. Peter's] now stands." (Courtesy American Antiquarian Society.)

[20] *PANORAMA OF SALEM* (1895 OIL PAINTING ON CANVAS BY ALBERT H. POOLE). Caught up in the bicentennial spirit of the witchcraft hysteria, druggists C.H. & J. Price commissioned Beverly Farms artist Bert Poole to create this panoramic scene of witches in flight to advertise their "delightful toilet requisite, "Witch Cream." The witch in the foreground is flying above Salem Willows, with the wharves off Derby Street in the background. Quizzical tourists almost always remark about the artist's inversion of the witches' broomsticks. (Courtesy Peabody Essex Museum.)

BONES OF GEO. JACOBS (C. 1971 PENCIL DRAWING). On May 2, 1783, Joseph Orne and Benjamin Goodhue dug up two finger bones, a coffin nail, and a pin on the former property of executed wizard George Jacobs, believing them to be from his grave site. A small, clear glass bottle with bright red sealing wax holds the cork stopper with ring handle in place, and a handwritten paper label was glued to the outer surface to identify the gruesome contents. This artifact was bequeathed to the Essex Institute in 1902 by Harriet P. Fowler.

[20] A WITCH STEALING CHILDREN (LATE-19TH-CENTURY POSTCARD). A mannish-looking, balding witch with a pronounced overbite, protruding proboscis, and large ear clasps two perplexed children as they speed along Salem Town with an ominous apocalypse-type cloud following in their wake. Tituba finally confessed that she "rid upon a stick or pole with Good and Osburn behind me." In his "Los Caprichos" series of macabre prints, Spanish artist Francisco de Goya (1746–1828) depicted two ugly nude women, one with black wings, flying through the firmament with a long cane and an affrighted cat on a serpent's tail. (Courtesy Peabody Essex Museum.)

[20] WITCHSTICKS, ONE OF A KIND (1992). Peter M. McSwiggin (right) presents one of his walking sticks to Dean T. Lahikainen, the Peabody Essex Museum curator of American Decorative Arts. McSwiggin gathered sticks from all the towns where the witchcraft victims resided, and handcrafted them to perfection. The founder of Witch City Enterprises also packaged "authentic soil from the hanging grounds of the Salem witches" in small plastic bags as souvenirs to sell for $2.95. (Courtesy McSwiggin Collection.)

[20] **An Ofrenda, Plummer Hall, the Phillips Library.** Mexicans have long celebrated deceased family members and friends with visually colorful and partially edible ofrendas (home altars) on "Todos Santos" (All Saints Day) and "Dia de las Animas" (All Souls Day), on November 1 and 2, respectively. The first colorful "Days of the Dead: The Arts of Los Muertos" exhibition was held in the Peabody Essex Museum's main facility in 1997, and future installations may also appear there.

[21] SALEM WITCH MUSEUM AND THE ROGER CONANT STATUE, 19 1/2 WASHINGTON SQUARE NORTH. Almost always mistaken for a witch or wizard, Roger Conant, Salem's founding father swathed in a flowing bronze cloak, greets visitors near the city's most popular witchcraft attraction. New York City architect Minard Lafever designed the Gothic Revival brownstone-and-brick edifice for the East Church (built between 1844 and 1846). Several years after its deconsecration, it housed the Salem Auto Museum, until the interior was destroyed by fire in 1969. Three years later Holly and Tom Mulvihill of Marblehead and White Oak Design created the Salem Witch Museum. Salem-born entrepreneur Biff Michaud (BPM Productions, Inc.) has owned the museum since 1980.

[21] PRAYERS AND FASTING, SALEM WITCH MUSEUM. Rev. Samuel Parris reads pertinent Biblical passages to his bed-ridden daughter, Betty, in the hope that words of the gospel, along with several days of fasting, will cure and take away the curse of witchcraft. Sculptor Nancy Sullivan created the polyester resin figures that appear in 11 scenes in a concentric arrangement to document with historical accuracy the unfolding events of the most infamous event in early American Colonial history.

[21] "MORE WEIGHT," SALEM WITCH MUSEUM. When spotlights are directed onto this vignette, individuals who know nothing about Giles Cory and his decision to remain mute under the weight of heavy stones are horrified. This type of cruel punishment was never again used in America.

[21] THE EXECUTION OF GEORGE BURROUGHS, SALEM WITCH MUSEUM. Adults and schoolchildren who have read or heard about the witchcraft delusion in Salem anticipate the final vignette as it is described by the authoritative voice of the narrator. Visitors leave the museum with a new understanding of the people and the period—able to correct others back home that burnings at the stake for witchcraft *never* occurred in Salem—and with a strong image of the phantasmagorical devil and the illuminated spiral on the floor with names and execution dates of the victims. Every evening interior lighting illuminates the arched Gothic windows, imparting a mysterious reddish-yellow glow to the impressive façade.

Four

FRIGHT SIGHTS

HAUNTED NEIGHBORHOOD, CORNER OF NORTH LIBERTY AND DERBY STREETS. One of the first references to a "haunted house" in Massachusetts appears in Cotton Mather's 1689 *Memorable Providences, Relating to Witchcrafts and Possesions*, regarding the aforementioned home of fellow Bostonian John Goodwin, where his four children had been bewitched the previous year. In 1831 another Boston author wrote that "numerous legendary tales were formerly propagated of haunted houses, where witches assembled and held their nightly orgies and diabolical revels. These haunts were always objects of great terror to the credulous vulgar, being considered as a pandemonium of all manner of evils, miseries, and calamities." By the end of the 1998 Hallowe'en season in Salem, a proliferation of haunted houses prompted some members of the city government to propose a ban on the future establishment of similar new businesses and "schlocky shops" to prevent the city from becoming too commercialized in that respect. (Courtesy Rick Wardell.)

Handwritten annotations on etching:
Deliverance Parkman's House 1670

Here, says Hawthorne, Alchemy was practiced.

DELIVERANCE PARKMAN'S HOUSE, 1670, FORMERLY LOCATED NEAR THE CORNER OF ESSEX AND NORTH STREETS (C. 1890 ETCHING BY LEWIS JESSE BRIDGMAN, 1857–1931). Picturesque may be the best adjective to describe this 17th-century structure with the lush vine engulfing most the clapboard-framed façade. First Period houses often feature impressive "HH" (Heaven and Hell) or HL (Holy Lord) wrought iron hinges on paneled doors that form a cross, in the belief that witches could not enter a double-crossed door. The rear view of the Parkman House supposedly served as the inspiration for the rear exterior of the House of the Seven Gables.

SPIRITS OF THE GABLES (1997). Historical interpreters dressed in mid-19th century-style clothing to represent Salem's most famous author, Nathaniel Hawthorne, and his cousin, Susannah Ingersoll, lead visitors through the House of the Seven Gables by candlelight on October weekends. An interactive play, *Spirits of the Gables*, explores the night shadows of the spooky 17th-century dwelling, and includes a visit by Matthew Maule's ghost. Family lunacy and deep secrets are dramatically revealed on the mystery tour. (Courtesy the House of the Seven Gables.)

THE HOUSE OF THE SEVEN GABLES, 54 TURNER STREET (C. 1938). In his famous romance novel of 1851, Nathaniel Hawthorne (1804–1864) wrote that the fictitious Matthew Maule "was one of the martyrs to that terrible delusion, which should teach us, among its other morals, that the influential classes, and those who take upon themselves to be leaders of the people, are fully liable to all the passionate error that has ever characterized the maddest mob. Clergymen, judges, statesmen, the wisest, calmest, holiest persons of their day, stood in the inner circle round about the gallows, loudest to applaud the work of blood, latest to confess themselves miserably deceived. If any one part of their proceedings can be said to deserve less blame than another, it was the singular indiscrimination with which they persecuted, not merely the poor and aged, as in former judicial massacres, but people of all ranks; their own equals, brethren, and wives." Built in 1668 for Capt. John Turner and Victorianized during the late 19th century (see p. 114), the structure was restored by Boston architect Joseph E. Chandler, under the aegis of local philanthropist Caroline O. Emmerton, and opened to the public in 1910. (Courtesy the House of the Seven Gables.)

COUNT KEN (C. 1983). A former employee of Dracula's Castle, Count Ken has been interested in extraterrestrial life for many years, and is probably Salem's first "Trekkie." In the late 1960s he founded the New England Saucer Research Club. Count Ken's 1983 poem "Lycanthropy" (in folklore, the magical power to transform oneself or another person into a wolf) includes these lines: "The sun is setting in the western sky; soon the harvest moon will be rising high. Once more the change will come over me—for I suffer the torment of lycanthropy." (Courtesy Ken Gilbert.)

DRACULA'S CASTLE, SALEM MARKET PLACE, BETWEEN FRONT AND NEW DERBY STREETS (1998 HANDBILL). Salem's first continuously operated haunted house, Dracula's Castle, features Bela Lugosi (1882–1956), star of the 1931 film *Dracula*, in its advertising; it invites visitors to "explore the dark hallways and eerie chambers . . . then have your picture taken in Dracula's coffin—if you dare!" Dracula's Castle has fun and thrills for the entire family.

"THE DOCTOR IS OUT . . . OF HIS MIND, THAT IS!" MAYHEM MANOR, 313 DERBY STREET.
Salem's newest fright sight is located in the research facility of the tragically departed Dr.
Morpheus Mayhem, who disguised his "clinic" as a tourist attraction to study people's reactions
to fear. Opened to the public in the fall of 1998, Mayhem Manor promises scares aplenty.
Dementio Dunham, one of the mad doctor's assistants, welcomes the brave of heart for a self-
guided tour of the sinister labyrinth, filled with paraphernalia that goes bump in the night.

**BORIS KARLOFF'S WITCH MANSION,
PICKERING WHARF.** Sarah, the daughter
of horror movie legend Boris Karloff
(star of *Frankenstein* in 1931), visited the
fright sight in October of 1998, saw the
3D Terror Vision show, tried chatting
with an "Elvira" look-alike, and inspected
the large cauldron, constructed for the
1985 animated Disney film *The Black
Cauldron.* Harry Houdini (1874–1926),
the celebrated stage magician and escape
artist, who may have known Boris Karloff
(1887–1969), coincidentally died on
Hallowe'en Eve, October 31, in the
tercentenary year of Salem's founding.

THE SALEM WITCH VILLAGE, 282 DERBY STREET. Petite employee and practicing witch Kelly T. O'Connor models a T-shirt of a witch praying to the moon at the entrance and gift shop area of "New England's only 'Haunted Neighborhood.'" During the month of October all the stops are pulled for the guided presentation through the interior maze of 12 scenes. Included in the miasma are blood-spurting fountains, enveloping fog, a gory graveyard depiction, macabre music, a headless horseman with his lively head, realistic animatronics, and slithering spiders descending from a 6-foot ceiling to ensnare arachnophobiacs. (Courtesy Wardell Collection.)

SAMANTHA'S BOUTIQUE, 205 ESSEX STREET MALL. The consignment boutique and costume shop owned by Sally Milo is not only "a bewitching place to shop," but is a frightening feast for the eyes each October, when interior and window designer Tom Greene of Danvers gets into the spirit of Hallowe'en with his colorful admixture of shimmering textiles and ghoulish accessories.

Five

HAUNTED HAPPENINGS

"HAUNTED HOUSE," AT THE "VOYAGE OF THE INDIAN STAR," PICKERING WHARF (1982).
Salem, Massachusetts, is the place to be during the month of October when the varied events
of "Haunted Happenings" take place. Originated in 1982 by co-chairs Joan P. Gormalley
(executive director of the Salem Chamber of Commerce) and Susannah Stuart (director of
the Salem Witch Museum), the now-almost-month-long festival is family oriented and yet
offers "treats" for all to share in the spirit of Hallowe'en. To ensure "good taste," the festival
committee of Haunted Happenings sent out a letter in 1983 in which they stated that "we
encourage all to participate in our [med-evil] costume competition and we require all costumes
to be original, a reflection of the evening's theme, and *in good taste* . . . Any person or persons
arriving at our festival clad in ugly, green-faced, troll-like, blood-dripped, or otherwise grotesque
costumes will *not* be admitted on the premises and *no* refunds will be given." (Courtesy Salem
Chamber of Commerce.)

A HAUNTED HAPPENINGS POSTER (1982). Haunted Happenings was begun as an antidote to the rash of accidents and poisoning scares perpetuated by sick adults who inserted razor blades and/or pins in apples and unwrapped candy bars for children going trick-or-treating. In 1982, about 60,000 visitors (daytrippers and "extra territorial tourists") flocked to Salem during the well-publicized last weekend in October. The success of the first Haunted Happenings is credited to cooperation between the business and cultural sections of the community, city officials, and the dedication of many volunteers. McDougall Associates, a local advertising agency that started in Salem, coined the festival name and designed the attractive poster. For more than a decade Parker Brothers Games funded the posters and accompanying brochures. (Courtesy Joan P. Gormalley.)

RONALD MCDONALD AND HIS MAGIC SHOW, EAST INDIA SQUARE (1982). Hamburger philanthropist Ray Kroc's famous clown delighted children and adults on Saturday morning with a magical performance in the foreground of the municipal parking garage. For $20 each, 40 grown-ups enjoyed a late-night "Insomniac's Tour," which began and ended at Hamilton Hall on Chestnut Street. The bus tour included admission to the Salem Witch Museum; a private candlelight performance by local storyteller Judith Black; a moonlight buffet at the Hawthorne Inn (which featured Bloody Marys and Eggs Tituba); and a presentation of *The Lord of Darkness* at the Barton Square Theatre. (Courtesy Salem Chamber of Commerce.)

THE SECOND ANNUAL PUMPKIN CARVING CONTEST, SALEM MARKET PLACE (1982 PHOTOGRAPH). The contest was held in the city's urban renewal area below the old town hall, between Front and New Derby Streets. Children who participated in the free event on Saturday afternoon had to BYOP (Bring Your Own Pumpkin and carving tools). Prizes were awarded for the most creative faces, and for the winners in the apple-bobbing contest. On Sunday evening, between 6 and 9 p.m., free rides were given to children in "The Great Pumpkin," a 75-foot glowing hot-air balloon at Pickering Wharf. (Courtesy Salem Chamber of Commerce.)

THE START OF THE "SPOOKY LIGHT WITCHES FLIGHT ROAD RACE" (1982 PHOTOGRAPH).
Mayor Jean A. Levesque officiates at the start of the 6.2-mile Saturday evening road race, sponsored by the Shawmut Merchants Bank and Historic Salem, Inc. For an entry fee of $4, runners could chase a "witch" through the streets, with 200 participants carrying special witch and cat-beamed flashlights. The invitation stated it would be "a scenic run starting at East India Mall in Salem's revitalized downtown, proceeding through its historic neighborhoods and along its waterfront, and finishing at the mall. Moderate hills." (Courtesy Salem Chamber of Commerce.)

A FRIGHT TRAIN POSTER. In an effort to control the increasing number of private vehicles arriving in Salem on October 31, and as an advertising gimmick, the Massachusetts Bay Transportation Authority recently inaugurated a "Fright Train." Popular with young families and high-spirited hobgoblins, the express train departs North Station in Boston at 6:15 p.m. and arrives in the "Witch City" in less than 25 minutes! In 1982 the Gray Line Bus Company offered a shuttle bus from Boston to Salem and back; the "Pumpkin Bus" left Copley Square at 9:30 a.m. and returned much too early at 3:30 p.m.

THE HORRIBLES' PARADE ALONG ESSEX STREET (1982). The second annual family-oriented parade "for children of all ages," started at town hall in Derby Square and followed part of the Heritage Walking Trail, a continuous red-painted line that passes by the stately Victorian buildings of the former Essex Institute, which presented "Salem Witchcraft: Documents of an Early American Drama." The "Monster Mash Hop" and the "Dracula Competition" at the Hawthorne Inn with "oldies" music helped celebrate the season. One could walk through "The Haunted Ghost Ship," which was docked at Pickering Wharf, or attend the "Bewitching Ball," sponsored by the Salem Witch Museum at Hamilton Hall, and win a $100 prize for the best costume. On Hallowe'en Weekend there was a "Psychic Festival" on the Essex Street Mall that included tarot card readings as well as a lecture series on ESP, reincarnation, the occult, and the significance of Hallowe'en. (Courtesy Salem Chamber of Commerce.)

HALLOWE'EN DOG CONTEST, SALEM COMMON (1997 OIL PAINTING ON CANVAS BY YETTI FRENKEL). Lynn muralist Yetti Frenkel took photographs of the most imaginatively dressed canines at the first annual dog contest and then incorporated them into a colorful panoramic painting with great appeal. Here, the artist is facing Washington Square East, while standing behind the Neoclassical bandstand, which was built in 1926 as part of the local tercentenary celebration. In the center of the painting, Briggs Street (named after Thomas Briggs) radiates from Salem Common (renamed Washington Square in 1802), on one of the largest public

spaces in New England. Flanking the street are the Greek Revival Nathaniel Silsbee Jr. House, built in 1832 (far left); the Nathaniel Silsbee House, built in 1818–19, and now owned by the Knights of Columbus; and the Dr. Hardy Phippen House, built in 1900 and now a funeral home (right). Miss Frenkel has included the twin stacks of the New England Power Company, and has judiciously eliminated the intricate *c*. 1850 cast-iron fence from the composition. (Courtesy of the artist.)

THE MORNING AFTER, NORTH LIBERTY STREET. Very early on November 1, the big clean-up by the city begins as a few tourists greet the new day and month. The exhibits in the museums will remain open through the Christmas season, but the fright sights tend to close up shop within the next few days; some, however, may entice post-Hallowe'en visitors on weekends with good weather. A gathering of city officials and business owners hold a debriefing to assess the quality of Haunted Happenings, the financial remuneration Salem will receive, and the revenue the delighted merchants need to carry most of them over until the following frightful season.

Six

SOME SALEM OCCULTISTS

SALEM ROSE AT DAWN (1993 OIL PAINTING ON CANVAS BY KATHLEEN WARD). From the studio in her Federal-period brick home facing Salem Common, where she was raised, former witch Kathleen Ward can dream up and paint mythical scenes with colorful images that transcend perceived reality. Ms. Ward described *Salem Rose at Dawn* as "a fantasy rendition of Salem overshadowed by the dread 'Devil in Massachusetts,' depicted in the fiery cloud formations over Derby Wharf. She stands witness to the 'Spirit of Truth,' beautiful, windswept but strong, despite the storm of controversy swirling overhead. Rose represents the soul of her people, encompassed by the light of heaven and having learned the lesson of love from that devastating tragedy that destroyed so many innocent lives at the hands of misguided zealots 300 years ago." (Courtesy of the artist.)

LAURIE CABOT WITH A FILM FRIEND AND HER DAUGHTER, JODY L. CABOT (1982). Born in Wewoka, Oklahoma, Laurie Cabot is the preeminent modern-day witch to become associated with Salem, after she moved to the city in the late 1960s. For the first Haunted Happenings weekend, she judged the children's costumes, and awarded a prize to a certain extraterrestrial. Ms. Cabot also presented "Casting the Circle" in the old town hall, and four years later she discussed the history of witches and modern magic with Phoenix School students. Hallowe'en marks the New Year for witches, and is a time for positive energy and good things, according to "The Official Witch of Salem." (Courtesy Salem Chamber of Commerce.)

Laurie Cabot
"The Official Witch of Salem"

Is Sharing Magic Through
LECTURE

Attend and understand that...

Everyone Is Psychic
No One Should Be Afraid
To Use Their Psychic
Abilities

Join her in discovering yours.

Date: October 28, 1987
Time: 8:00 pm
Where: Old Town Hall
          Salem, MA

Only $12.00 per person

Public Welcome

To Benefit The Witches' League For Public Awareness

A LAURIE CABOT LECTURE POSTER (1987). One of Ms. Cabot's raison d'etre is the education of people about her followers and others who practice Wicca (an Anglo-Saxon word meaning "wise one"). Shortly after her 16th birthday, Laurie realized that she was a witch, and that witchcraft is "very beautiful, very powerful . . . We consider it an art, a religion, and a science." She later took a vow to wear long black robes to honor the Wiccan god and goddess. This provocative clothing, her flowing tresses, and accentuated make-up (including the recently tattooed azure blue spiral on her left cheek that symbolizes the help and guidance derived from the ancient ones) sets Laurie Cabot apart as a unique individual. (Courtesy Theriault Collection.)

94

SALEM'S CELEBRATED WICCAN (C. 1986 PHOTOGRAPH). On Samhain (pronounced "sow-ane"), the evening of October 31, the Black Doves of Isis, under Laurie Cabot's protective wings, march to Gallows Hill in a candlelight procession to commemorate their civil rights and to remember friends who have passed on to another level. Witches regard Samhain as a High Holy Day, and it has been the New Year of the Celts for countless centuries. In her Book of Shadows—a personal memoir and book of instructions kept by most who practice Wicca—Laurie Cabot noted that in 1986 she founded the Witches' League for Public Awareness. In 1973 she opened "A Witch Shop" at 100 Derby Street in Salem, followed by Crow Haven Corner at 125 Essex Street in 1975, which she then gave to her daughter Jody in 1979. Laurie's third shop, The Cat, The Crow & The Crown, is located at Pickering Wharf, and is where she gives consultations, autographs her three books, and offers religious ephemera for sale. (Courtesy Laurie Cabot.)

SORCERESS SHAMAN (1992 WATERCOLOR BY LINDA WEINBAUM). This feathered fantasy was included in the first one-woman psychic art exhibit in Salem, called "Sacred Spaces," at O'Flaherty's on Central Street. Proprietor John Flaherty now operates the Salem Tea Room and The Fool's Mansion (a Medieval and Gothic-inspired clothing shop). The civil rights of some witches in Salem were threatened by a band of fanatic religious fundamentalists in 1992, but the state's attorney general, Scott Harshbarger, warned them to desist. Witchcraft is a verified religion, as are more traditional forms of religion.

A MAGICK BOOK QUEST, CROW HAVEN CORNER, 125 ESSEX STREET. In search of a special grimoire (a book of magick formulae) to add to his library of the occult, Thomas L. Creamer of Lynn prepares to enter Salem's witch shop garbed in a star-studded black robe with blue stars and a vine-wrapped walking stick. The shop sells amulets, plastic pouches of magical powders, and an assortment of polished stones and prismatic crystals.

AN IN-HOUSE READING AT THE SALEM TEA ROOM, 96 WHARF STREET, PICKERING WHARF. In lieu of reading tarot cards, internationally known licensed psychic and medium Linda Weinbaum reads tea leaves and crystals (as did her great-aunt, Leah Goldminz, at age 92) for Dianne Digris, manager of the psychic tea room. The bejeweled dragon-box on the table is an example of Linda's intuitive ceramic artwork, which is shown in galleries throughout New England. Executed witch Samuel Wardwell was known to be a fortune teller in Salem Village, and in 1884 local clairvoyant Mrs. Lydia M. Buxton advertised in the city directory that she was a "business and test medium."

OFFERING A LIBATION IN HIS HOME.
A former student of Laurie Cabot, Andrew W. Jackson Jr., H.P., is a high priest of Wicca who began the Coven of the Shadows of the Sanctuary in Salem in 1990. His chosen name, "White Hart of the Coombe," came to him while on a visit to the English countryside. Well known in the greater Wiccan community and in Salem as "one of the mystics in town," White Hart is an herbalist, an aromatherapist, and a professional psychic. His "magickal" skills are being passed on to his attentive students in the coven, currently known as "House of Sweet Life" (an Egyptian term for school).

A REFLECTION OF DIANA, SALEM'S PSYCHIC CENTER, PICKERING WHARF. The crystal ball Diana McKanas is holding in the 1983 photograph is one she has used in her psychic profession for about 30 years, 18 of which while practicing in Salem. Aura readings, astrology, meditation, polarity healing, and spiritual counseling are some of the areas of expertise Diana uses as an internationally known psychic.

Exorcising the Demons (1992). Reformed Salem witches Paula Gauthier (left) and Kathleen Ward pose in front of some spiritually dramatic paintings shown in their studio exhibition, "Contemporary Iconography & Occult Ritual Abuse 'Survivor' Art." From left to right are Mrs. Gauthier's *Marantha* and *Pelican in the Wilderness* (both painted in 1992), and *Deliver Me From Evil* (1989). (Courtesy of the artists.)

Aroma Sanctum Perfumes in The Fool's Mansion, 127 Essex Street. Impish Akuura Kulak is mixing a magical perfume for a regular customer in the aromatherapy section of John Flaherty's colorful cloak-and-dagger emporium. Nicholas Culpepper's *The English Physition Enlarged: Medicine Made of English Herbs* (1681) is from the same period as the John Ward House, which was built after 1684 and is on the grounds of the Peabody Essex Museum. If available to Mrs. Ward, it may have inspired her to plant a small herb and flower garden such as the one adjacent to the lean-to of the venerable dwelling.

MUSICIANS FOR THE NEW MILLENNIUM. For their initial CD, *Book of Shadows*, Teisan Russell and Amanda Adams recorded 13 haunting songs for Akashic Records in Salem; the cover features a mystical symbol and "Coven 13," their band's name. Regarding the title song, Wiccan high priest Shawn Poirier, the duo's spiritual mentor, has written "Each one of us casts varying degrees of light and shadow by which the Book of our life is written and rewritten over, and over yet again until the day comes when All is known and the shadows are laid to rest . . . Forever!" Teisan Russell, the mesmerizing lead singer and lyricist, resides in Salem near Gallows Hill, and Amanda Adams, his alluring composer and classically trained accompanist, is a native of the South Shore of Massachusetts. (Courtesy Akashic Records.)

Seven

PAGEANTS, PLAYS, AND FILMS

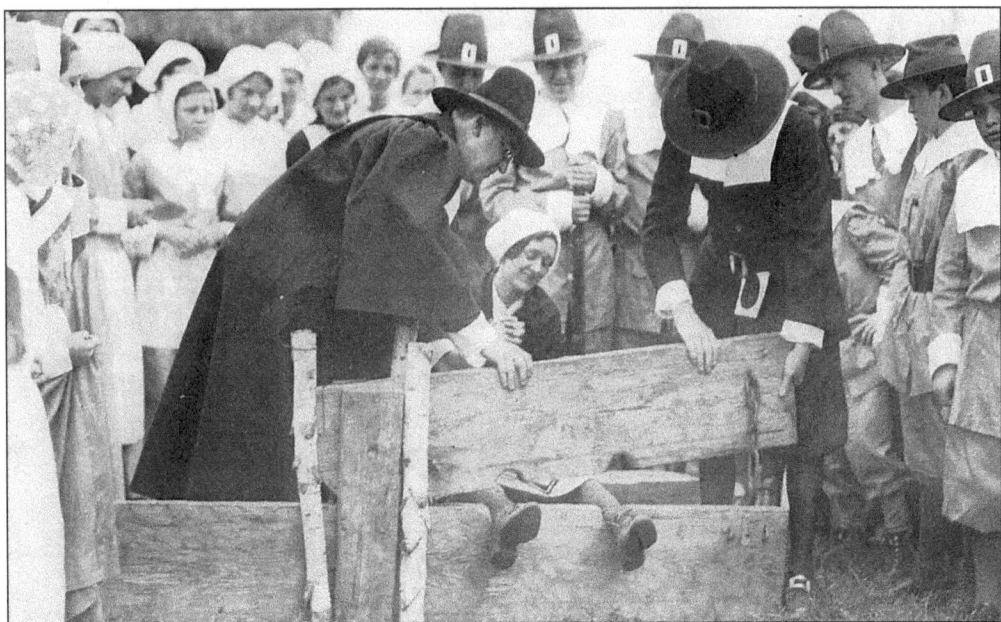

THE PUNISHMENT FOR VAIN PRIDE, PIONEER VILLAGE, FOREST RIVER PARK (JUNE 12, 1930). A bewildered but nonetheless bold woman is about to be secured by officials in the town's stocks for defying Gov. John Endecott when he reprimanded her for flaunting a bright red scarf. Bemused onlookers in "The Village Episodes" pageant crowd around the scene of her public humiliation. Having one's feet locked in the stocks, or standing with one's head and hands restrained in the pillory, made offenders think twice about committing crimes again. The pageant at Pioneer Village attracted over 20,000 people for the opening of the recreated outdoor living history museum, which celebrated the rigors of daily life in Salem during the first settlement. Sixty-odd years later, after the last executions for witchcraft in Salem Town, the General Court prescribed a more lenient sentence for those who continued to practice witchcraft—offenders had to spend six hours in the pillory, four times a year, with a year in jail. (Courtesy Theriault Collection.)

"BEWITCHED" (C. 1965 COMIC BOOK COVER BY SCREEN GEMS, INC.). The local weather in late June of 1970 must have been bewitched, as it played havoc with the 32 members of the cast and crew of the popular ABC television comedy while they were in the city to shoot six special episodes of the "Salem Saga." Many citizens tried to catch glimpses of Elizabeth Montgomery (Samantha), Dick York's replacement, Dick Sargent (Darrin), and Agnes Moorhead (Endora), while they were in residence at the Hawthorne Inn. "Bewitched" was undoubtedly inspired by the 1942 Universal film *I Married a Witch*, starring Veronica Lake. (Courtesy Pickering Wharf Antiques Gallery.)

SALEM CHRONICLES (1972 BOOK COVER BY BALDWIN DESIGN). The stark statue of Salem's founder Roger Conant inspired playwright Robert Murray to script a "theatrical scenario" of the city's historical highlights as a wake-up call "to dramatize the error and waste of urban renewal." Begun in 1964 by the Salem Redevelopment Authority, early plans threatened the demolition of architecturally significant Federal-period brick buildings in the Derby Square area. On the opening night in February at the old town hall "Everything paused in absolute stillness while a white-haired Salem lady [Helen Usher, a Chestnut Street grande dame], with astonishing simplicity created the bafflement of Rebecca Nurse . . ." (Courtesy Jim and Helen Baldwin.)

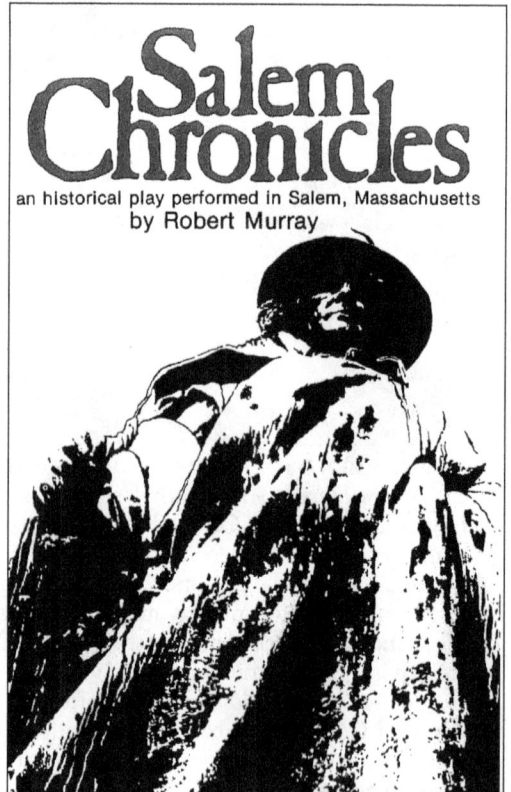

"Salem Ghosts," a Dramatization Held at the Old Town Hall, 32 Derby Square (1982). Salem's original "haunted house" was designed and built on the second floor of the 1816 brick structure by Jack O'Connor, Mark Sarto, and Bruce Whear, and was sponsored by the chamber of commerce and the East India Mall. The "eerie experience" turned out to be quite controversial because an unexpected mushroom-shaped cloud appeared in the finale. Levitation, as witnessed in 17th-century Salem Village, occurred when Margaret Rule was seen to levitate from her bed and could not be held down, as recalled by six townsmen. (Courtesy Salem Chamber of Commerce.)

Sarah Cloyce's Painful Memories (1985 photograph). Witchcraft survivor Sarah Cloyce of Salem Village (portrayed by Vanessa Redgrave) is comforted and steadied by her nephew, Samuel Nurse (Ron Hunter), before telling of the horrendous events of 1692, including her solitary confinement and deprivation in an Ipswich jail. Upon hearing her story, three bewigged Boston magistrates gave Sarah three gold sovereigns for her suffering and for the loss of her dear sisters, Rebecca Nurse and Mary Esty; the coins were supposedly buried with the sickly Mrs. Cloyce shortly thereafter. (Courtesy Nightowl Productions.)

SAMHAIN ALTAR AT GALLOWS HILL (1992). Essex County filmmakers Joe Cultrera, Henry Ferrini, Phil Lamy, Bob Quinn, and John Stanton combined their skills over a six-year period to produce *Witch City*, a quirky documentary about the commercialization of the Salem witch trials. The "down home" quality of Salem in the 1950s is contrasted with the later hucksterism and clashes between local witches (who were celebrating Samhain) and religious fundamentalists during the tercentenary year of 1992. In the film, the "Witch City" logo of a crone flying on a broomstick is shown as both a harmless symbol and a derogatory representation. (Courtesy Henry Ferrini.)

TITUBA'S TERROR (1992 PHOTOGRAPH FROM THE PLAY *SALEM'S DAUGHTERS*). Fear of the hangman's noose overcomes Rev. Samuel Parris' slave Tituba (performed by Autumn Saunders) in the second-year run at Salem State College of Cambridge playwright Wendy Lement's play, which was directed by David Allen George. Ms. Lement expanded one scene into a 20-minute production she called *Tituba's Tale*, which was first performed the previous year in the vacant room of a building at Pickering Wharf. (Courtesy Prof. David Allen George.)

"Hocus Pocus Domenocus," Ropes Mansion, 318 Essex Street (1992). Paula B. Richter, assistant curator of the former Essex Institute and resident curator of the Ropes Mansion (Memorial), poses by the front entrance of the late-1720s Georgian-style mansion, which has been decorated in the spirit of Hallowe'en for the Walt Disney Pictures film *Hocus Pocus*. The illuminated front windows of the house and the flickering faces of the jack-o-lanterns made a big impression on those who witnessed the nocturnal filming. Also used as a setting for the 1993 film, which starred Bette Midler, Sarah Jessica Parker, and Kathy Najimy, was the former Phillips School on Washington Square South. (Courtesy Elwin R. Richter.)

A Confrontation with the Devil (1992 photograph from the film *Nathaniel Hawthorne's Young Goodman Brown*). While traveling far into the mysterious forest one night, Goodman Brown (Tom Shell) encounters the "Prince of Darkness" (John P. Ryan) dressed as a local villager, who tempts him with material and sensual pleasures. Nathaniel Hawthorne's 16-page 1835 short story inspired Peter George, a director and writer, and Robert Tinnell, a producer, to join forces in transforming the Gothic romance (filmed at Brooksby Farm in Peabody, the Rebecca Nurse Homestead, and Pioneer Village in Salem) into "the best interpretation of Hawthorne ever to come to the screen." (Courtesy 50th Street Films/Troma, Inc.)

NEWLY MADE FRIENDS FROM 1692 (OCTOBER 1995). Incredibly beautiful weather prompted these extras in the 1996 Twentieth Century Fox film *The Crucible* to enjoy many lunchtime breaks on an adjacent hill on Hog Island in Ipswich Bay. Intermingling with stars Daniel Day-Lewis, Winona Ryder, and Paul Scofield are, from left to right, an unidentified woman, Mike Neary, Lucia Ravens, Deborah Lathrop, Dianne Law, and Davis Griffith. Concurrent filming took place on the island owned by the Trustees of Reservations and in a vacant building on the grounds of the former United Shoe Machinery Corporation in Beverly, now the Cummings Center. (Courtesy Deborah Lathrop.)

A PERTINENT AUTOGRAPH (1995). Pulitzer Prize-winning playwright Arthur Miller inscribes one of his books for Andrew Messersmith of Essex, who was hired as an extra for the film *The Crucible*, and who worked as the animal coordinator. For his important play based on the life and death of John Proctor Sr. and his "jade," Mr. Miller in 1952 did his research of original witchcraft documents at the Essex County Courthouse and the Essex Institute. Modern-day inspiration for the play revolved around the "witch hunts" in February of 1950 by Sen. Joseph McCarthy, who wanted to expel "Communists" from the State Department. (Courtesy Robert V. Brophy.)

Eight

FRIGHTFUL FIENDS
AND FRIENDS

FRIGHTFUL FIENDS AND FRIENDS (1984). Most of these pranksters disporting themselves in the lobby of the Hawthorne Inn were then residing in the greater Boston area, but visited Salem each Hallowe'en for the annual costume ball. For a $5 per person admission fee to the grand ballroom, hobgoblins could shake their bones to rock n' roll music, purchase a libation at the bar, and delight in each others' company and costumes between the respectable hours of 8 p.m. and midnight. Regarding what may have been the first "Hallowe'en costumes" written about in late-17th-century New England, Ann Putnam Jr. described in vivid detail "two women in winding-sheets, and napkins about their heads, at which I was greatly affrighted. And they turned their faces . . . and looked very red and angry [and then they] looked as pale as a white wall." (Courtesy Mary A. Cheever.)

A Brotherly and Sisterly Costumed Group, 138 Federal Street (1968). Seated on the front lawn of the former Assembly House (now the Cotting-Smith-Assembly House) are, from left to right, David Gaudrault, Laura Hunt, Johnathan Hunt, and Susan Gaudrault. The Hunt family lived for 10 years as house custodians at the 1789 historic residence. (Courtesy Donald F. and Elizabeth S. Hunt.)

A Laurie Cabot Costume Ball Poster (1975). Laurie Cabot initiated the annual Witches' Ball in Salem in 1971. Twelve years later, on October 30, 1983, the Witches of New England presented "A Witches' Festival and Pageant" at the Hawthorne Inn from 9 p.m. to 1 a.m. Music was provided by "Wheel of the Year" (Gypsy and a Band of Witches). There was a Medieval costume competition, Renaissance music, and a Harvest Buffet sponsored by Salem State College, all for a donation of $15 per person. (Courtesy Theriault Collection.)

A KNIGHT TO REMEMBER, SEA WITCH GIFT SHOP, 143 DERBY STREET (C. 1985 PHOTOGRAPH). Ted Knight, the genial news anchor on TV's "The Mary Tyler Moore Show," poses with Sophie B. and Henry R. Theriault while visiting the North Shore. A former tour guide for the city, Henry Theriault is an indefatigable collector of Salem ephemera, and for the past 26 years has been the proprietor of the fascinating gift shop near the Salem Maritime National Historic Site Orientation Center. A font of local information, Henry is his own chamber of commerce, and always welcomes each visitor to his shop with two friendly questions: "Where are you from?" and "Have you got a good map of the city?" (Courtesy Thaddeus Buczko.)

"I'LL GET YOU MY PRETTY . . ." (1987). Mary Cheever, a resident of Lynn and an employee of Gebelein Silversmiths at 286 Newbury Street in Boston, chats with a life-size witch used as a store advertisement at Jamie Russell's Gift Shop at 270 Essex Street, not far from the Witch House. There is a strong indication that Mary's ancestor was Ezekiel Cheever, a tailor who served as the court reporter of the witchcraft trials.

BANKERS' HOLIDAY, HERITAGE CO-OPERATIVE BANK, 71 WASHINGTON STREET (1989 PHOTOGRAPH). Employees of the people-friendly bank, which is located near the site of the first courthouse in Salem, have been "dressing up" for Hallowe'en for more than a decade. Bank patrons look forward to the last weekend of October to see what the theme will be. Erected *c.* 1882 by an unidentified architect, the bank was established the following year, and remodeled a second time (after 1910) in the Colonial Revival style. The architecturally rich interior features an octagonal domed ceiling with arched windows, festooned urns, and a balustrade. (Courtesy Heritage Co-operative Bank.)

"WHO IS THAT FACE IN THE MASK?" (1988). Bedazzled by the London production of Andrew Lloyd Webber and Cameron MacIntosh's *Phantom of the Opera*, Salemite Robert F. Gilbert dons a look-alike mask, black cape, and clutches a carnival cane while peering mysteriously through the frame of a Chippendale looking glass. On the staff in the radiology department of the North Shore Medical Center, Bob is a descendant of John Symonds, the early-17th-century Salem joiner (former term for cabinetmaker) who emigrated from Great Yarmouth, Norfolk, England, before 1636. Sarah W. Symonds, the early-20th-century bas-relief sculptor, was also a relative.

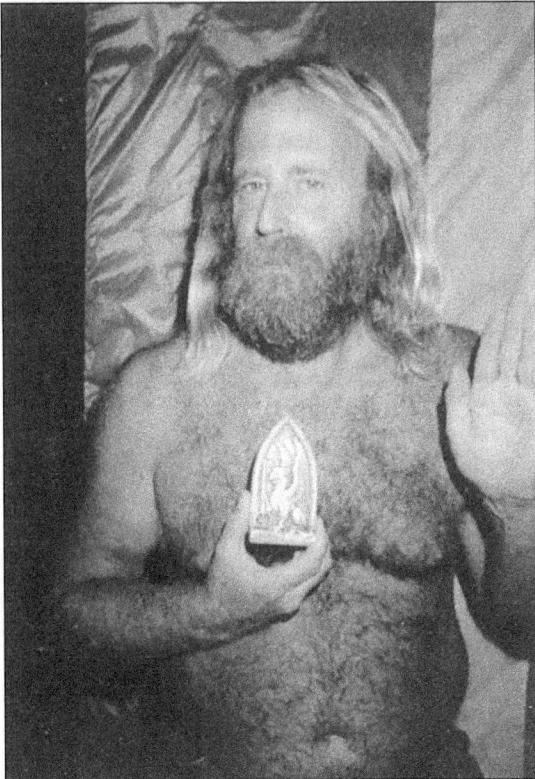

BEWARE THE GRIFFIN! (1998). Lynn naturist Dave Lent chose a mythological plaster cast reproduction for this image taken by David Dunham Sr. of Salem at his "little shop of auras," located at Mayhem Manor. Scientific biofeedback imaging and the capturing of a person's aura in polychrome hues is a specialty of his business, "Dagas." In 1692 Tituba told magistrate Hathorne that one of the devil's familiars was "all over hairy (as is Mr. Lent), all the face hairy, with a long nose . . ." and who wore black clothes. (Courtesy of the photographer.)

MIMICKING AN EDVARD MUNCH SCREAM, 7 RIVER STREET. For more than 20 years Salem attorney John H. Carr Jr. has carved several gigantic pumpkins in the front yard of his home, much to the delight of his three sons, their neighbors, and all who happen upon this magical nocturnal experience. Half a dozen friends transported the approximately 2,479-pound quartet of large "Cucurbita pepos" on trucks from the Topsfield Fair. John used a variety of knives for the pre-sunrise sculpting. Thirty to forty tall white candles flicker inside each pumpkin, and child-size reproduction gravestones with amusing names abound. (Courtesy John H. and Carol Carr.)

Nine

HALLOWE'ENIANA

A PUMPKIN MAN AND JACK-O-LANTERNS (20TH CENTURY). Grimacing pumpkin faces reflect some of the spookiness of the Hallowe'en season, and examples such as these are very collectible. Classified as a "veggie person," the modern standing figure with movable arms was made of a resin paper composition and hand-painted in a limited edition of 2,500 (or less) by Debbie Thibault's American Collectibles, Hawaiian Gardens, California. The early-20th-century paper mâché pumpkins fortunately retain their inserted printed paper faces. Other sought-after Hallowe'en objects include embossed German die-cuts, celluloid and hard plastic figures and toys, hand-painted and transfer-printed ceramics, noisemakers, candy containers, chocolate and ice cream molds, costumes and masks, games and souvenirs, and paper ephemera including postcards. (Courtesy Richard D. Wright, right.)

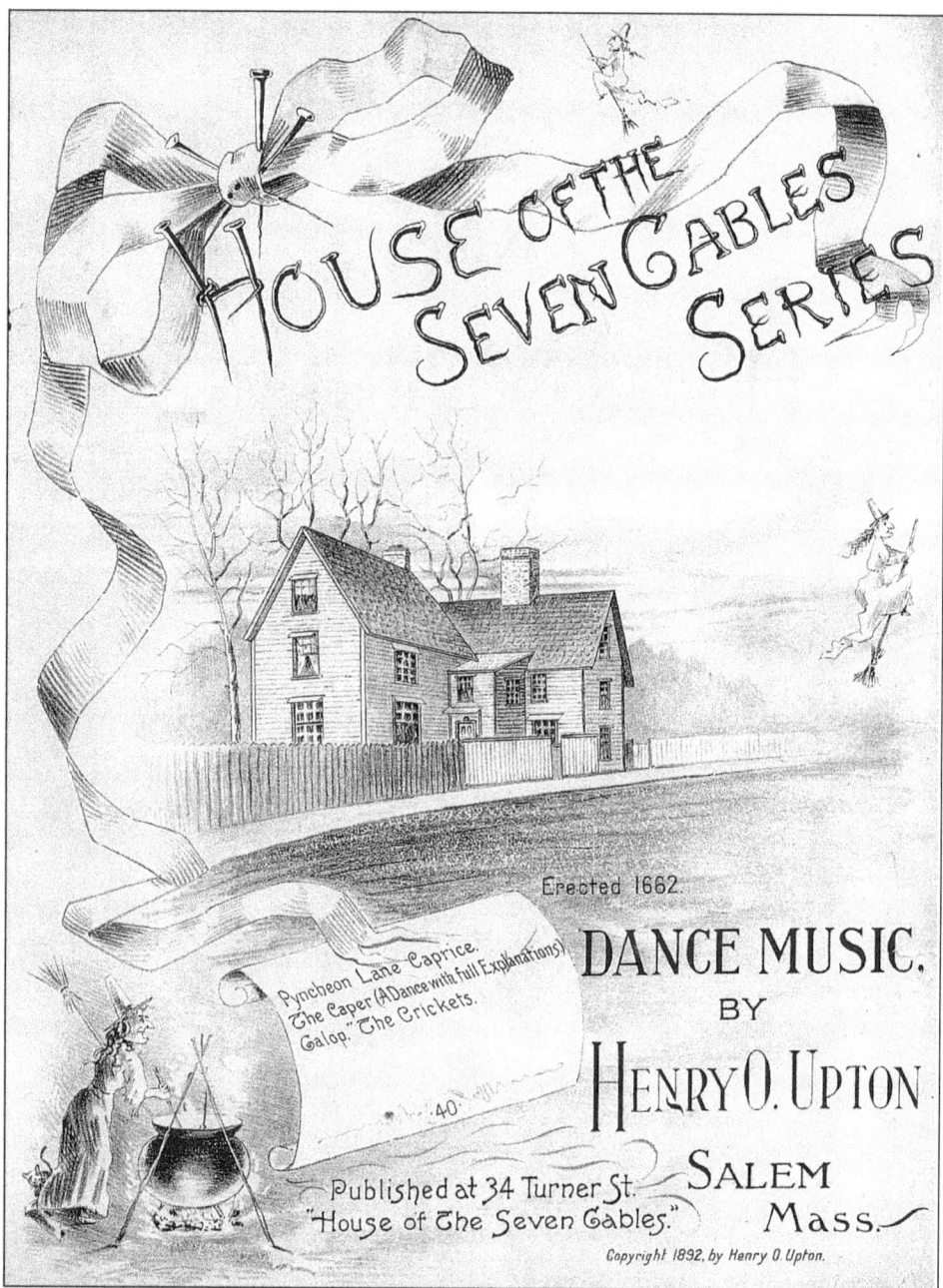

SHEET MUSIC COVER (1892). Bent "witch pins" form the letters of the title of the dance music and secure the bowknot of the decorative ribbon, while sister witches stir a large cauldron and fly by and over one of the most famous houses featured in American literature. Composer Henry O. Upton was the last private owner of the "Gables," and it was he who discovered the "secret staircase" that leads from the richly paneled dining room to a small third floor room, now known as Clifford Pyncheon's bedchamber. Located at the foot of Turner Street next to Salem Harbor, the historic dwelling had this appearance until it was restored between 1908 and 1910. (Private Collection.)

THREE GLASS BOTTLES (C. 1890 TO C. 1920). These bottles feature a witch to advertise the liquid contents. Ephraim Provo's light amethyst bottle was pressed at 4/6 Sewall Street. The Salem Chemical Company's 4-ounce light green bottle with printed paper label was manufactured at their 2 Walter Street factory, and J. Edward Hennessy's clear glass bottle, which contained "Witch City Drinks," was made at the former Provo firm from 1908 until 1921.

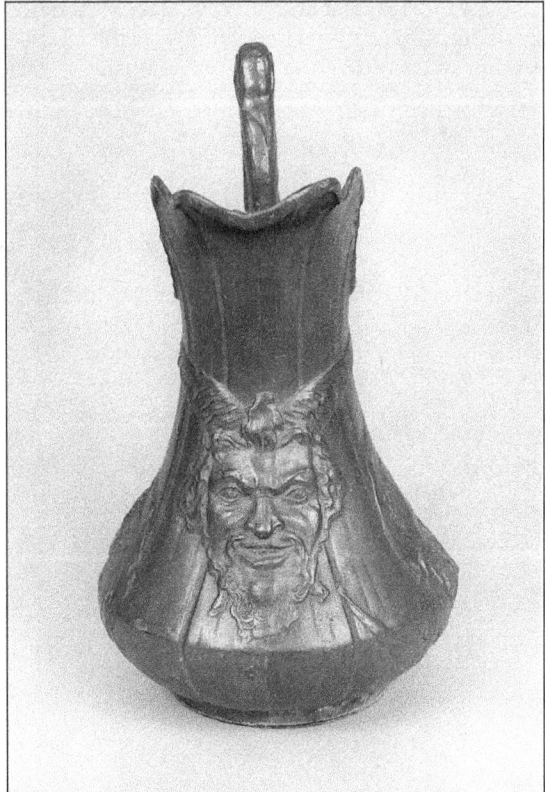

A WATER PITCHER WITH DEVIL MASK (C. 1900 PEWTER VESSEL MADE BY "KAYSERZINN"). A repoussé diabolical mask dominates this utilitarian object, which features German bearded irises in the Art Nouveau style on the fluted sides. The Deutschland factory was founded in 1874 in Krefeld, and was under the direction of designer Hugo Leven when the sinuous forms of the turn of the 20th century were fashionable.

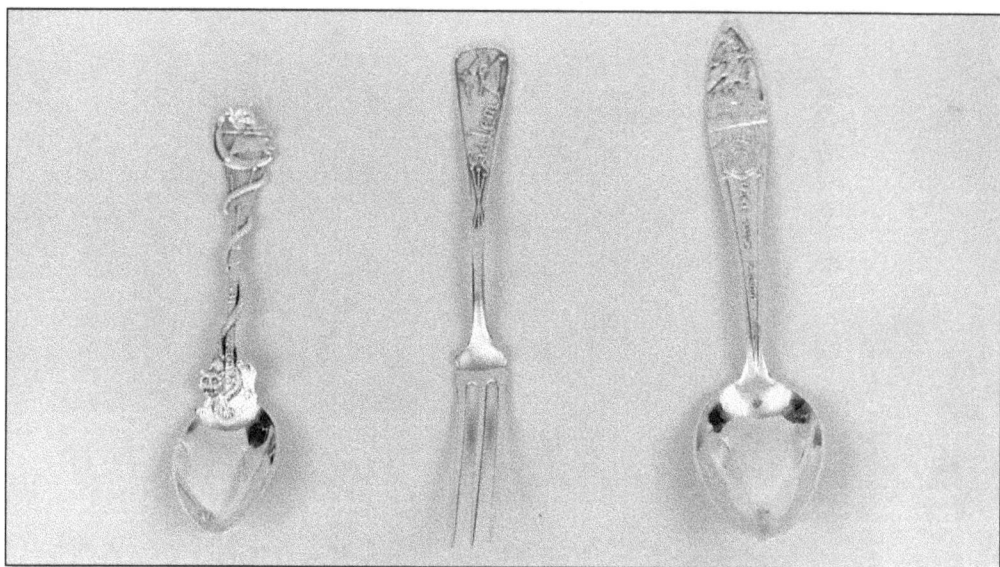

THREE WITCH SOUVENIR STERLING SILVER EATING UTENSILS (LATE 19TH/EARLY 20TH CENTURY). The "interesting mania" for collecting souvenir spoons was initiated by Daniel Low & Company, which was located at 231 Essex Street until 1995. Their first "Witch" pattern, shown on the pickle fork, was patented on March 3, 1891, and appears on various pieces initially made by the William B. Durgin Company of Concord, New Hampshire. The second pattern was introduced in 1893, and is shown at the left on a teaspoon made by the Gorham Manufacturing Company of Providence, Rhode Island. A later variant is the pierced-handled spoon incorporating a witch flying over the House of the Seven Gables and the city seal, which was manufactured by the Watson Company of Attleboro, Massachusetts.

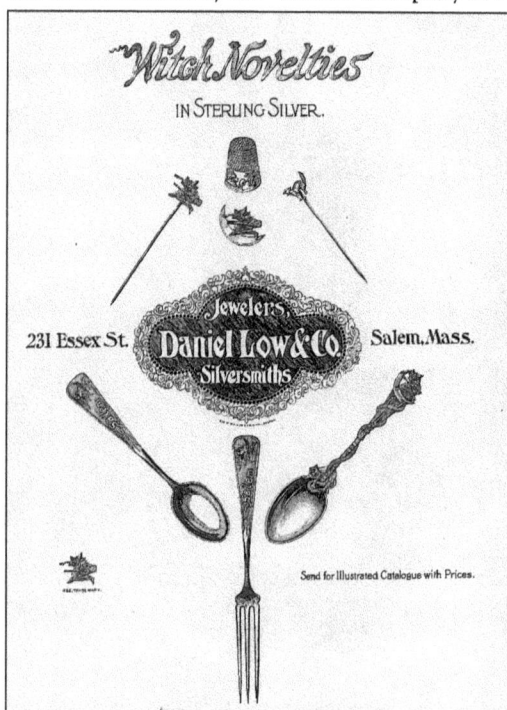

WITCH NOVELTIES ADVERTISEMENT (C. 1908 BACK COVER OF THE "MARCH OF THE SALEM WITCHES" SHEET MUSIC). Popular novelties in sterling silver, and some with leather, included baby spoons, bonbon boxes, bookmarks, brooches, cat's head scarf pins, charms, cuff buttons, English Crown Lavender Salts, hat pins, match boxes, pencil tips, pen wipers, pocket cribbage boards, rattles (with pearl rings and silver bells), salve boxes, stamp cases, stocking darners, thimbles, etc. Prices during the first decade of the 20th century ranged from 25c per bookmark to $5.50 for a pair of 14K gold cuff links. (Courtesy Theriault Collection.)

116

MIRROR-IMAGE WITCHES (EARLY 20TH CENTURY). The transfer-printed blue-and-white ceramic plate and the acid-etched pewter plate, manufactured by Frank Beardmore & Co., Fenton, England, and hand-crafted by Reed & Barton for Daniel Low & Co., respectively, are identical examples of the same witchcraft design being used by different firms to sell popular souvenir items. During the late 19th and early 20th century, Austrian, English, and German porcelain-making manufacturers produced countless souvenirs relating to "witches" and local sites of historical interest. Steins made in Germany usually only bear inventory numbers, and unpainted "blanks," which could be hand-painted by talented artists such as Ida Upton Paine of Salem, were made by T & V (Limoges) in Touraine, France.

A WITCH "300" PUZZLE (C. 1900). The Salem Chemical and Supply Company used their trademark to decorate the cover of this art picture puzzle. "Ye Witchcraft Game," a family card game introduced by Parker Brothers in 1890 and discontinued in 1894, is extremely rare. The Parker Brothers firm was established in 1888 by George S. Parker, and for over 100 years it was located on Bridge Street opposite the granite-block jail. Monopoly, the firm's first real estate board game with its small wooden buildings and paper money, was the most popular product it introduced.

HALLOWE'EN PRECAUTIONS (C. 1909 POSTCARD). Some of the traditional symbols and colors of Hallowe'en include a witch on a broomstick flying in front of a golden crescent moon, an arched-back black cat, and jet-black bats flying over a harvested cornfield with bright, or burnt, orange pumpkins. A rare albino owl would be a treat to see any evening. (Courtesy Theriault Collection.)

A HALLOWE'EN MISS PAPER DOLL (C. 1920). Eleanor Broadhead, while residing at 124 Federal Street with her parents, Frederick W. and Edith Perkins Balch Broadhead, and her sisters, Elizabeth and Marjorie, collected this festively attired paper doll, which was printed in the *Ladies Home Journal*. At her examination on March 1, Tituba told Judge Hathorne that red and black rats "as big as a little dog" scratched her after she said a prayer, telling her to "Serve them" and to do "more hurt to the children." (Courtesy Eleanor Broadhead.)

Oct. 31st (C. 1910 POSTCARD PUBLISHED IN GERMANY). The last evening in October is known as "Nutcracker Night" in England, as nuts were used to foretell the future before being devoured. During the 1840s Irish immigrants to America brought their own Hallowe'en folkways, which included bobbing for apples and lighting jack-o-lanterns. The leader of "the flock of cackling birds" on the postcard is holding her besom (a broom made of twigs with a handle) with a cord as the trio prepares to land in the frog-infested pasture that was deeded to Rev. Samuel Parris by Deacon Ingersoll. (Courtesy Theriault Collection.)

A PLASTER PLAQUE OF A FLYING WITCH (C. 1906 BAS-RELIEF SCULPTURE BY SARAH W. SYMONDS). Miss Symonds, a Salem-born bas-relief sculptor of plaster and cast-iron decorative and functional objects with local themes, had her first studio on the second floor of the John Ward House, and resided nearby at Ives Court off St. Peter Street. Between 1918 and 1953, Miss Symonds' "Colonial Studio" was in the Bray House at 1 Brown Street, where she made and sold her composition material plaques, many of which were given an "ivory finish." The largest flying witch plaque (18 by 29.5 inches) sold for $10, and the 2.5-inch circular ones retailed for 25c apiece. (Courtesy Theriault Collection.)

119

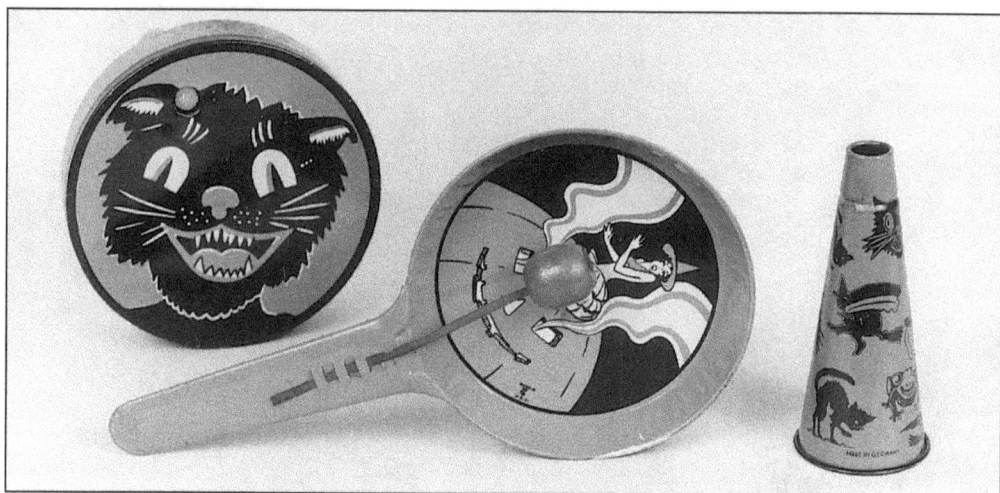

METAL NOISE MAKERS (EARLY 20TH CENTURY; MADE IN AMERICA AND GERMANY). Printed tin noise makers helped yesterday's children to scare away ghosts and goblins by rotating a cat-faced ratchet-type toy; by banging a wooden ball against a frying pan-type toy with a sorceress atop a pumpkin; and by signaling each other with a cone-type horn with various Hallowe'en symbols. (Courtesy Robert and Carol Swift, left.)

THREE LIGHTING DEVICES (20TH CENTURY). This illuminating trio includes a wax pumpkin candle with a witch's hat, a battery-operated hard plastic lantern, and a decal-and-painted metal chamberstick. In his small *c.* 1930 booklet "Quaint Gifts from Olde Salem," Harold L. Cassino, owner and manger of The Cassino Studio at 144 Washington Street, advertised a "Hand Decorated Salem Witch Hearth Brush [which] is a real reproduction of an old timer. Very strongly made. An attractive novelty. Cost $1.50," and "The Witch Foot Scraper. A novel and useful article [a witch on her hands and knees astride a broom]. Gray iron. Cost $2.50." (Courtesy Marla Bryerlynne Segal Collection, far left; Schier Collection, middle.)

CRESCENT MOON DIE-CUTS (C. 1915; MADE IN GERMANY). A pair of orange-and-black crescent moon-shaped die-cuts feature an eye-to-eye jogging pumpkin and a bat with a six-pointed star. The circle is an ancient symbol, and the most important one in the Craft of Wicca, as it represents the retaining of energy. The colors of Samhain, red or black, are represented by circular fruits such as apples, pomegranates, and pumpkins. (Courtesy Richard D. Wright Collection.)

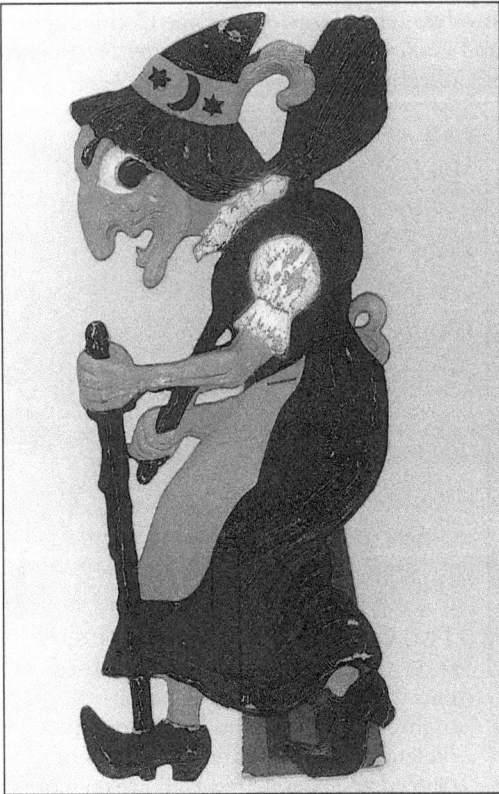

A PERAMBULATING WITCH DIE-CUT (C. 1920; MADE IN GERMANY). The down-turned nose and chin of this crone are mirrored in her up-turned pointed shoes. German die-cuts were very popular collectibles when they were introduced to the American market around 1910, and they are more so today; the designs were stamped-out in different sizes, with this witch being one of the largest (15.5 inches).

TWO COMPOSITION FIGURES AND A "CAULDRON" (C. 1930S–1940S; MADE IN GERMANY). A toothy witch and a black cat with large yellow eyes flank a cast-iron Cape Cod lighter to represent a witch's cauldron. Cauldron Court and Gallows Hill Road are nearby on Salem's most infamous hill. (Courtesy Richard D. Wright Collection.)

TWO CREPE PAPER HATS (C. 1940S; MADE IN JAPAN). Similar superimposed hats display circular stickers of a frightened black cat and a contorted skeleton with very whimsical bands of pierced and silhouetted Hallowe'en motifs.

CELLULOID AND PLASTIC WITCH TOYS (C. 1930S, C. 1950; MADE IN AMERICA). The weighted and balancing celluloid egg was produced by the Viscoloid Company of Leominster, Massachusetts, and the hard plastic witch and pumpkin on a motorcycle was manufactured by the E. Rosen Company. Approximately 1,000 motorcyclists arrived at Pickering Wharf one Sunday afternoon in late October of 1998 on the last stop of their annual charity ride called the "Harley Witch Ride," to support the Muscular Dystrophy Association. (Courtesy Marla Bryerlynne Segal Collection, left, and Richard D. Wright Collection.)

CRYSTAL FORTUNES (C. 1940; MADE BY H.E. LUHRS, AMERICA). An equal number of boys' and girls' fortunes can be revealed on this printed cardboard game by spinning the wheel to the right side of the sorceress. (Courtesy Bunny Gorfinkle.)

A NEON WITCH, SALEM BEER WORKS, 278 DERBY STREET (C. 1950s). Illuminated upon request in the dining area, this vitriolic bright-green neon witch was made as a trade sign by and for the Salem Sign Company, which was located at 230 Highland Avenue. She now flies over the names of beers and ales served in the restaurant. Some beverages with Hallowe'en, or local names, are Black Bat Stout, Pumpkin Head Ale, and Witch City Red. In 1982 bartenders from the greater Boston area competed in the "Witches' Brew Taste-Off" in Victoria Station at Pickering Wharf with their own recipes, all of which were made with KAHLÚA.

GRAVESTONE SHADOWS (© 1962 PEN-AND-INK POINTILIST DRAWING). Christian More's slate gravestone in the Old Burying Point is one of the earliest surviving in a Salem cemetery to feature a winged death's head. The English translation of the Latin epitaph above her name, "HODI MIHI CRAS TIBI," is "Today for me, tomorrow for you." Richard More was a passenger on the *Mayflower* when it landed first in Provincetown and then in Plymouth, Massachusetts, in 1620. His unadorned, simple gravestone is near that of his wife.

"TRICK OR TREAT?" (1979 SCHERENSCHNITTE BY CLAUDIA HOPF). Nineteenth-century Pennsylvania German paper-cutting was revived by Ohio native Claudia Hopf around 1966. Her son Perry cuts the paper with small surgical cornea scissors, and then she uses watercolors for the positive areas while the background receives black paper for contrast. Not visible is a complementary grained frame made by her husband, Carroll. While they were living in Salem, Claudia wrote in her on-going diary in May of 1985 that she "watched the first episode of *Three Sovereigns for Sarah*, the tale about witchcraft hysteria, [and she exclaimed] It is very good!" (Private Collection.)

THE SAMUEL PICKMAN HOUSE, NORTH LIBERTY STREET (1975 WOOD ENGRAVING BY ELEANOR MEADOWCROFT). The Buckinghamshire-born folk artist whose surname means "keeper of a meadow" in England, created this detailed print of a Colonial maid in the stylized garden of the pre-1681 house owned by the Peabody Essex Museum. Restored in 1970 by Phillip Budrose, the peaked-roofed structure retains original fireplace, door, and wall closet trim in the earliest chamber. The gravestones in the foreground of the print are where the Salem Witch Trials Memorial is located. (Private Collection.)

125

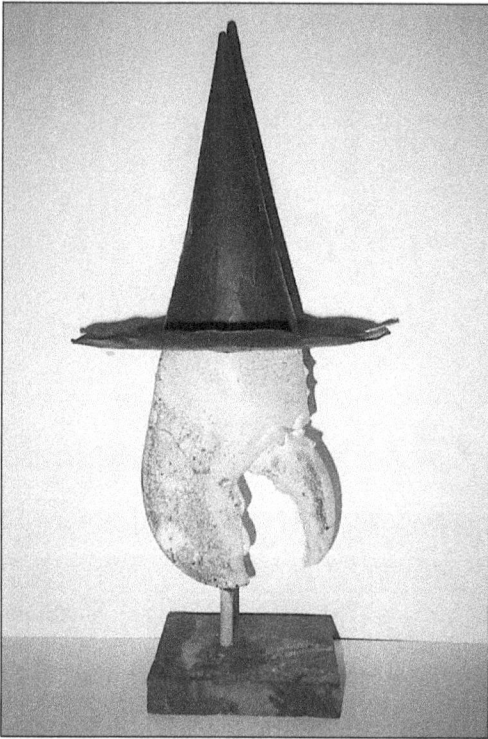

LOBSTERWITCH (C. 1991 SCULPTURE BY RACKET SHREVE). The winner of the 1990 Massachusetts Waterfowl Stamp Competition created this fanciful sculpture from a large lobster claw and a cardboard hat painted matte black. One of the Shreve family tombs in Harmony Grove Cemetery in Salem had unfortunately been vandalized, prompting Racket to retrieve a section of a wooden coffin for the base of the lobsterwitch! (Courtesy of the artist.)

A BICYCLE RACE POSTER (1984). In 1899 "Salem Witch Cycles," a bicycle company established by Robert H. Robson, advertised for the first time in the *Salem City Directory*. A witch in flight has been a visible part of the masthead of *The Salem Evening News* for innumerable decades. The high school football team sports the nickname the "Salem Witches," and in 1971–72 the Witchcraft Heights Elementary School was built in the Gallows Hill area. Although deeply resented by contemporary practitioners of Wicca, the more than century-old symbol of a Salem witch in flight remains a visible part of the city's lore and lure, and is apparently here to stay. (Courtesy Schier Collection.)

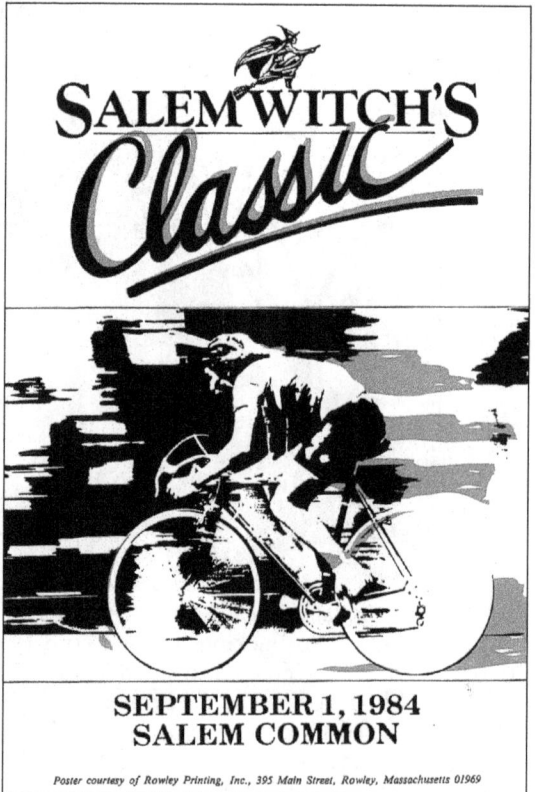

SALEM WITCH'S Classic

SEPTEMBER 1, 1984
SALEM COMMON

Poster courtesy of Rowley Printing, Inc., 395 Main Street, Rowley, Massachusetts 01969

UNIFORM PATCH (C. 1995). Chief of Police Robert M. St. Pierre designed the official emblem, which also appears on police vehicles and those of the fire department. The blue field has a black witch silhouetted against a white night sky as she flies across the yellow crescent moon; all the letters are light yellow, with the exception of "1626" (the year of Salem's founding), which is black. (Courtesy Salem Police Department Collection.)

PICTURE PUZZLE: FIND TWO HEADS
REPRODUCED FROM AN OLD WOODCUT SHOWING AN ORIGINAL SALEM WITCH AND ONE OF HER PRETTY VICTIMS.

A CLIPPER SHIP INN POSTCARD (C. 1983). This provocative picture puzzle is thought to have been first sold at Elizabeth Balch's "The Old Salem Corner Studio" in Hamilton Hall in the 1930s. The inscription on the reverse of the image states: "The witches of New England were reputed to be the craftiest in the world, possessing through a mystical process of optical illusion the power to make themselves invisible, although plainly in sight. Can you see the witch?" (Courtesy Schier Collection.)

BIBLIOGRAPHY

Boyer, Paul and Stephen Nissenbaum. *Salem Possessed, The Social Origins of Witchcraft*. Cambridge, Massachusetts, and London, England: Harvard University Press, 1974.

Brown, David C. *A Guide to the Salem Witchcraft Hysteria of 1692*. Worcester, Mass: Mercantile Printing Co., 1984.

————, (editor). "The Salem Witchcraft Trials: Samuel Willard's Some Miscellany Observations," in *Essex Institute Historical Collections* (hereinafter referred to as *EIHC*), July 1986.

Burr, George Lincoln. *Narratives of the Witchcraft Cases*. New York: Charles Scribner's Sons, 1914.

Cave, Alfred A. "Indian Shamans and English Witches in Seventeenth-Century New England," in *EIHC*, October 1992.

Cummings, Abbott Lowell. *The Framed Houses of Massachusetts Bay, 1625–1725*. Cambridge, Massachusetts, and London, England: The Belknap Press of Harvard University Press, 1979.

Dailey, Barbara Ritter. "Where Thieves Break Through and Steal: John Hale Versus Dorcas Hoar, 1672–1692," in *EIHC*, October 1992.

The Diary of William Bentley, D.D. Gloucester, Mass: Peter Smith, 1962.

Gildrie, Richard P. "The Salem Witchcraft Trials as a Crisis of Popular Imagination," in *EIHC*, October 1992.

Gragg, Larry D. "Samuel Parris: Portrait of a Puritan Clergyman," in *EIHC*, October 1983.

Hansen, Chadwick. *Witchcraft at Salem*. New York: George Braziller, 1969.

Hill, Frances. *A Delusion of Satan*. New York: Da Capo Press, 1997.

Kamensky, Jane. "Words, Witches, and Women Trouble: Witchcraft, Disorderly Speech, and Gender Boundaries in Puritan New England," in *EIHC*, October 1992.

Peabody, George, Esq. *Account of the Centennial Celebration in Danvers*. Danvers, Mass: printed by order of the town, 1852.

Perley, Sidney. *The History of Salem, Massachusetts, Vol. III*. Salem, Mass: Sidney Perley, 1928.

Proper, David R. "Salem Witchcraft, A Brief History," in *EIHC*, July 1966.

Richardson, Katherine W. *The Salem Witchcraft Trials*. Salem, Mass: Essex Institute, 1983.

Roach, Marilynne K. "That Child, Betty Parris: Elizabeth (Parris) Barron and the People in Her Life," in *EIHC*, January 1988.

Rosenthal, Bernard. *Salem Story*. Cambridge, United Kingdom: Cambridge University Press, 1993.

Starkey, Marion L. *The Devil in Massachusetts*. New York: Alfred A. Knopf, 1950.

Tapley, Harriet Sylvester. *Chronicles of Danvers*. Danvers, Mass: The Danvers Historical Society, 1923.

Thacher, James. *An Essay on Demonology, Ghosts and Apparitions. Also, an Account of the Witchcraft Delusion at Salem in 1692*. Boston, Mass: Carter and Hendee, 1831.

Tolles, Bryant F. Jr., *Architecture in Salem*. Salem, Mass: Essex Institute, 1983.

Weisman, Richard. *Witchcraft, Magic, and Religion in 17th-Century Massachusetts*. Amherst, Mass: The University of Massachusetts Press, 1984.